greatitalianfood

greatitalianfood

The Australian Women's Weekly cookbooks

contents

italian essentials

The characteristic simplicity of most Italian food is due to a few versatile, yet tasty, ingredients forming the basis of many delicious recipes. Following is a guide to those most widely used.

parmesan

There are two types of Italian parmesan: **Parmigiano Reggiano** and **Parmigiano Pedano**. Reggiano is usually aged for three years, giving it a harder texture and a stronger, more mature flavour than Pedano. It also tends to be cheaper and more readily available.

Parmesan is best bought in a block, and grated as required, as pre-grated parmesan quickly loses its flavour.

mozzarella

Mozzarella is a soft, elastic cheese, stretching into long strands when heated. It is used most often on pizzas, but can also be sliced and included in salads, or toasted in cheese sandwiches.

It was originally made from buffalo milk, which can still be bought at specialty cheese shops, but it is now mostly made from cow milk.

Bocconcini are small balls of fresh mozzarella, stored in whey. They must be eaten within a day or two of purchase and refrigerated, covered, in a container of water. **Baby bocconcini** are tiny balls of bocconcini, and are lovely when halved and tossed into a salad.

mortadella

A soft-textured, smoked sausage with a mild flavour. Mortadella is made with pork fat, veal and beef, and flavoured with spices and often pistachios.

pepperoni

A long, thin, Italian-style salami made with pork, beef and added fat. Pepperoni is seasoned with ground red capsicum and is relatively spicy.

polenta

Polenta refers to both cornmeal and the dish made from it. Add dry polenta to boiling salted water or stock and stir until thick and smooth. Butter and parmesan can be added for extra flavour.

Eat polenta as is, or pour into a baking dish, cool, cut into squares and grill or fry. Polenta makes a pleasant change from rice and mixes well with Mediterranean flavours and roasted meats or vegetables.

prosciutto crudo

Sometimes called parma ham, this is a salted and air-cured ham, perfectly safe to eat raw. It is usually cut paper-thin and eaten with figs or slices of melon as a starter or part of an antipasto platter, but it can also be grilled or fried until crisp. Prosciutto cotto (cooked ham) is also available at some delicatessens.

pancetta

Pancetta has a distinctive red colour, and it is one of the most popular cured meats. It comes from the flesh found directly under the skin around the pig's stomach. Each type of pancetta is prepared with salt and pepper, however some varieties also incorporate various spices.

focaccia

This bread is usually made in a rectangular shape. It grills beautifully and is just the right thickness and texture for a grilled open sandwich. Cut the focaccia into a chunk, halve it, toast it lightly and pile on chopped salami, olives, sun-dried or fresh tomatoes, anchovies, sliced artichoke hearts and cheese. Grill for a few minutes to warm and melt the cheese, and you have the perfect lunch or snack.

ciabatta

focaccia

ciabatta

Meaning 'slipper' in Italian, this flat, oval bread is slightly crunchy on the outside with a soft, chewy interior. The bread is light and porous and the flavour is delicately sour.

mozzarella

parmigiano reggiano

bocconcini

parmigiano pedano

baby bocconcini

romano

pepato

provolone

cheddar

fontina

smoked cheddar

gorgonzola

ricotta

goat cheese

cream cheese

fetta

mascarpone

Italians love cheese and use it in many of their recipes. Apart from their huge and diverse range of local cheeses, they have also enthusiastically embraced the cheeses of France, Britain and Greece.

to cook pasta

dried pasta

Gradually add pasta to a large saucepan of boiling water, making sure water does not go off the boil. When cooking 'long' pastas, such as spaghetti, hold strands at one end until the submerged end becomes soft in the water. Gradually lower strands, coiling them neatly. Cook pasta until just tender; it should be 'al dente' (to the tooth) – tender but firm.

Cooking times for pasta will vary according to individual manufacturers so check pasta regularly to ensure it does not overcook.

Pasta should only be rinsed after draining if being used in a cold dish, or not being served immediately. In these cases, rinse pasta under cold running water to stop the cooking process, then drain.

Uncooked dried pasta can be stored up to a year in a cool, dry place. Cooked pasta can be refrigerated, covered, for 3 days.

fresh pasta

Fresh pasta is cooked in much the same way as dried pasta, however it requires much less cooking time.

Gradually add fresh pasta to a large saucepan of boiling water, making sure water does not go off the boil. Allow to cook for a few minutes until pasta is "al dente". It will not take long, so check pasta regularly to ensure it does not overcook.

why is pasta so good?

Pasta is usually made from wheat flour or semolina and water. It is a great source of carbohydrates and is fortified with folic acid, which may protect against certain cancers and heart disease. The complex carbohydrates give slow-release energy, making it popular amongst athletes and also good for diabetics. There is less than half a gram of fat in a 1/2-cup serving of pasta, so it is perfect for those watching their weight.

pasta shapes

It is important to choose a pasta shape to complement your sauce. Generally, long, thin pastas suit light, thin sauces; thicker pastas suit heavier sauces; smaller shapes with ridges or holes are perfect for chunkier sauces; and small pastas, such as risoni and macaroni, are good in soups.

We have specified a pasta for each recipe, however if you prefer, simply substitute any pasta of your choice.

come si dice?

Use this list of pronunciations to project your 'knowledge' of fine Italian cuisine:

amaretti - *(am-ah-REHT-tee)*
antipasto - *(ahn-tee-PAHS-toh)*
arborio rice - *(ar-BOH-ree-oh)*
arrabbiata - *(ar-rah-BEE-ah-tah)*
balsamico - *(bal-SAH-mih-koh)*
biscotti - *(bee-SKOH-tee)*
bocconcini - *(bohk-KOHN-chee-nee)*
bruschetta - *(broo-SKEH-tah)*
cacciatore - *(kah-CHUH-tor-ee)*
calzone - *(kal-ZOH-nay)*
cannoli - *(kan-OH-lee)*
cappuccino - *(kap-poo-CHEE-noh)*
carpaccio - *(kahr-pah-CHEE-oh)*
conchiglie - *(kon-KEEL-yeh)*
crostini - *(kroh-STEE-nee)*
espresso - *(ehs-PREHS-oh)*
fettuccine - *(feh-TAH-chee-nee)*
focaccia - *(foh-kah-CHEE-ah)*
gnocchi - *(NYOH-kee)*
gorgonzola - *(gohr-guhn-ZOH-lah)*
gremolata - *(greh-moh-LAH-tah)*
lasagne - *(luh-ZAHN-yuh)*

mascarpone - *(mas-kahr-POH-nay)*
minestrone - *(min-NES-TROHN-nay)*
mozzarella - *(moht-SUH-REHL-lah)*
orecchiette - *(oh-rayk-KEE-EHT-tay)*
osso buco - *(AW-SOH BOO-koh)*
pancetta - *(pan-CHEH-TUH)*
panforte - *(pan-FOHR-tay)*
parmigiano - *(pahr-MEE-jar-noh)*
penne - *(PEN-nay)*
pepato - *(peh-PAH-toh)*
pizza - *(peet-ZUH)*
primavera - *(PREE-mah VEHR-ah)*
prosciutto - *(proh-SHOO-TOH)*
ricotta - *(rih-KOH-TUH)*
saltimbocca - *(sahl-TIHM-boh-KUH)*
tiramisu - *(tih-ruh-mee-SOO)*
torrone - *(toh-ROHN-nay)*
tortellini - *(tohr-TL-EE-nee)*
vermicelli - *(ver-ma-CHEL-ee)*
zabaglione - *(zah-bahl-YOH-nay)*
zuccotto - *(zoo-KOHT-toh)*
zuppa inglese - *(zoo-PUH ihn-GLAY-zay)*

spaghetti

pappardelle

green and
yellow fettuccine

penne

curly lasagne

rigatoni

tagliatelle

green
and white
tortellini

gow gee wrappers

small
spirals

lasagne sheets

bow ties

antipasto

Traditionally served as an appetiser, a range of delicious antipasto is available, ready to serve, from large supermarkets or delicatessens. An appealing selection, as shown in this platter, should ideally include both purchased and homemade items, with as wide a range of tastes and textures as possible. Choose from a selection of cured meats (salami, mortadella, prosciutto); vegetables (roasted tomatoes, marinated eggplant, mushrooms and artichoke hearts, peeled capsicum, herbed olives); crunchy Italian breadsticks known as grissini; and cheeses (marinated bocconcini, baked ricotta, wedges of gorgonzola and perhaps a hard cheese, such as parmesan).

marinated olives
with rosemary and thyme

PREPARATION TIME 10 MINUTES (plus marinating time) ■ COOKING TIME 5 MINUTES

200g green olives, drained
200g black olives, drained
2 tablespoons fresh thyme
⅓ cup fresh rosemary
2 cloves garlic, sliced thinly
2½ cups (625ml) olive oil
½ cup (125ml) lemon juice

1 Layer olives, herbs and garlic into hot sterilised 1-litre (4 cup) jar.

2 Gently heat oil and juice in medium saucepan; do not boil. Pour enough of the oil mixture into jar to cover olives, leaving 1cm space between olives and top of jar; seal while hot.

makes 4 cups

per serving 17.3g fat; 727kJ

store   Recipe best made 3 days ahead; can be refrigerated for up to 3 months.

tip   Oil will solidify on refrigeration; bring to room temperature before serving.

marinated eggplant

PREPARATION TIME 15 MINUTES (plus standing and marinating time) ■ COOKING TIME 10 MINUTES

10 baby eggplants (600g)

coarse cooking salt

1 litre (4 cups) white vinegar

2 cups (500ml) water

1 tablespoon coarsely chopped fresh mint

1 teaspoon dried thyme

1 clove garlic, sliced thinly

1 fresh red thai chilli, seeded, chopped finely

1/2 teaspoon ground black pepper

1 1/2 cups (375ml) hot olive oil

1 Quarter eggplants lengthways; place in colander. Sprinkle with salt; stand 1 hour. Rinse eggplant under cold running water; drain on absorbent paper.

2 Heat vinegar, the water and 2 teaspoons of the salt in large saucepan until hot; do not boil.

3 Add eggplant; simmer, uncovered, 5 minutes. Drain; discard vinegar mixture.

4 Combine herbs, garlic, chilli, pepper and oil in large heatproof bowl.

5 Place eggplant upright in hot sterilised 1-litre (4 cup) jar. Carefully top with enough oil mixture to cover eggplant, leaving 1cm space between eggplant and top of jar; seal while hot.

makes 40 pieces

per serving 2.8g fat; 128kJ

store Recipe best made 3 days ahead; can be refrigerated for up to 3 months.

deep-fried whitebait

PREPARATION TIME 10 MINUTES ■ COOKING TIME 15 MINUTES

1 cup (150g) plain flour
¼ cup coarsely chopped fresh basil
1 teaspoon garlic salt
500g whitebait
vegetable oil, for deep-frying

spiced mayonnaise dip
1 cup (300g) mayonnaise
2 cloves garlic, crushed
2 tablespoons lemon juice
1 tablespoon drained capers, chopped finely
1 tablespoon coarsely chopped fresh flat-leaf parsley

1   Combine flour, basil and garlic salt in large bowl. Toss whitebait in flour mixture, in batches, until coated.

2   Heat oil in medium saucepan. Deep-fry whitebait, in batches, until browned and cooked through; drain on absorbent paper. Serve with spiced mayonnaise dip.

spiced mayonnaise dip   Combine mayonnaise, garlic, juice, capers and parsley in small serving bowl.

serves 4

per serving   48.1g fat; 2966kJ
tip   Serve as a starter, or present on a platter as finger food for a party.

anchovy suppli

PREPARATION TIME 20 MINUTES (plus cooling time) ■ COOKING TIME 40 MINUTES

2 cups (400g) medium-grain rice

2 teaspoons olive oil

90g canned anchovy fillets in oil, drained, chopped finely

2 cloves garlic, crushed

2 tablespoons tomato paste

1 tablespoon finely chopped fresh parsley

2 tablespoons finely grated parmesan cheese

125g mozzarella cheese, cut into 1cm cubes

plain flour

2 eggs, beaten lightly

1 cup (100g) packaged breadcrumbs

vegetable oil, for deep-frying

tomato sauce

1 trimmed stick celery (75g), chopped finely

1 small brown onion (80g), chopped finely

1 clove garlic, crushed

1/2 cup (140g) tomato paste

1 1/2 cups (375ml) water

1 Cook rice in large saucepan of boiling water, uncovered, until just tender; drain.

2 Heat olive oil in small frying pan; cook anchovy, garlic, paste and parsley until fragrant. Combine rice and anchovy mixture in large bowl with parmesan. Mix well; cool.

3 Flatten a level tablespoon of the cooled rice mixture in one hand; top with a cube of mozzarella. Cover mozzarella with another level tablespoon of the rice mixture.

4 Carefully shape rice mixture or suppli into balls. Coat suppli in flour; dip in egg, then breadcrumbs. *[Can be made a day ahead to this stage and refrigerated, covered.]*

5 Heat vegetable oil in large saucepan; deep-fry suppli, in batches, until golden brown. Drain on absorbent paper. Serve suppli with tomato sauce.

tomato sauce Cook celery, onion and garlic in heated small non-stick frying pan, stirring, until celery is soft. Stir in paste and the water; bring to a boil. Reduce heat; simmer, uncovered, about 15 minutes or until sauce thickens. *[Can be made 2 days ahead and refrigerated, covered, or frozen for up to 3 months.]*

serves 6

per serving 17.8g fat; 2184kJ

little fried cheese pastries

PREPARATION TIME 30 MINUTES (plus standing time) ■ COOKING TIME 35 MINUTES

1½ cups (225g) plain flour

½ cup (75g) self-raising flour

1 tablespoon olive oil

¾ cup (180ml) beef stock

¼ cup (50g) ricotta cheese

⅓ cup (40g) grated smoked cheddar cheese

½ cup (50g) grated mozzarella cheese

⅓ cup (25g) grated parmesan cheese

50g thinly sliced salami, chopped finely

1 egg white, beaten lightly

1 tablespoon finely chopped fresh rosemary

pinch ground nutmeg

vegetable oil for deep-frying

1 Sift flours into large bowl; make well in centre. Pour in a small amount of combined olive oil and stock. Using one hand, work in flour a little at a time. Gradually add stock mixture, working in flour until mixture comes together in a ball.

2 Press mixture together to give a firm dough. Knead dough on lightly floured surface about 5 minutes or until dough is smooth and elastic. Cover dough with slightly damp cloth; stand 5 minutes.

3 Meanwhile, combine cheeses, salami, egg white, rosemary and nutmeg in medium bowl; mix well.

4 Roll dough on lightly floured surface until as thin as possible. Cut into 5cm rounds. Cover with slightly damp cloth to prevent dough drying out.

5 Place 1 level teaspoon of the cheese mixture in centre of each round. Brush edges of rounds with a little water. Place another round on top of cheese mixture; press edges together firmly.

6 Heat vegetable oil in large saucepan; deep-fry pastries, in batches, until browned. Drain on absorbent paper.

makes 45

per pastry   2.6g fat; 209kJ

seafood platter

PREPARATION TIME 30 MINUTES (plus marinating time) ▪ COOKING TIME 20 MINUTES

500g baby octopus

500g medium uncooked prawns

12 scallops

300g calamari rings

300g piece firm white boneless fish, chopped coarsely

300g piece salmon

¹/₂ cup (125ml) olive oil

¹/₄ cup (60ml) balsamic vinegar

¹/₄ cup (35g) finely chopped, drained sun-dried tomatoes

2 tablespoons finely chopped fresh oregano

2 cloves garlic, crushed

1 tablespoon lime juice

3 uncooked balmain bugs (350g), halved

12 small black mussels (250g)

1 Remove and discard heads and beaks from octopus; cut each octopus into quarters. Shell and devein prawns, leaving tails intact.

2 Combine octopus, prawns, scallops, calamari, fish and salmon in large non-reactive bowl with oil, vinegar, tomato, oregano, garlic and juice; mix well. Cover; refrigerate 3 hours. *[Can be made a day ahead to this stage.]*

3 Remove octopus, scallops, calamari, fish and salmon from marinade. Cook, in batches, on heated oiled grill plate (or grill or barbecue), uncovered, until browned all over and just cooked through. Slice salmon.

4 Remove prawns from marinade; discard marinade. Cook prawns and bugs on grill plate until browned both sides and just changed in colour. Cook mussels on grill plate until shells open; remove and discard half of each shell.

5 Serve seafood on one large platter or individually.

serves 6

per serving 26.4g fat; 2070kJ

bagna cauda

PREPARATION TIME 5 MINUTES ■ COOKING TIME 20 MINUTES

2²/₃ cups (600ml) thickened cream

60g butter

45g can anchovy fillets, drained, chopped finely

2 cloves garlic, crushed

1 Place cream in small saucepan; bring to a boil. Reduce heat to low; simmer, uncovered, about 15 minutes or until cream thickens, stirring frequently.

2 Meanwhile, melt butter over low heat in medium saucepan, taking care not to brown butter. Add anchovy and garlic; stir until mixture is blended well and becomes paste-like.

3 Stir hot cream into anchovy mixture until well combined; serve warm.

makes 2³/₄ cups

per tablespoon 9.5g fat; 370kJ

tip Traditionally served warm, you can serve bagna cauda in a fondue pot with a small tea light or gentle flame underneath. Serve with your favourite selection of crisp vegetables.

marinated mushrooms

PREPARATION TIME 15 MINUTES (plus marinating time)

¼ cup (60ml) lemon juice

½ cup (125ml) olive oil

¼ teaspoon salt

1 teaspoon finely chopped
  fresh tarragon

2 tablespoons finely chopped
  fresh parsley

250g button mushrooms,
  sliced thinly

1 Combine juice, oil, salt, tarragon and parsley in medium non-reactive bowl; mix well. Add mushrooms; mix well. Cover; marinate mixture 4 hours or overnight. *[Can be made 2 days ahead to this stage.]*

2 Using slotted spoon, remove mushrooms from marinade.

serves 4

per serving 28.7g fat; 1133kJ

tip Marinated mushrooms are delicious tossed through a green salad.

marinated calamari

PREPARATION TIME 25 MINUTES (plus refrigerating and marinating time) ·
COOKING TIME 15 MINUTES

500g calamari rings
⅓ cup (80ml) lemon juice
⅓ cup (80ml) olive oil
1 clove garlic, crushed
1 tablespoon finely chopped fresh parsley

1 Drop calamari into large saucepan of rapidly boiling water; reduce
   heat. Simmer about 10 minutes, or until calamari is tender; drain.
   Combine juice and oil in medium non-reactive bowl; add calamari.
   Cover; refrigerate overnight. *[Can be made a day ahead to this stage.]*

2 Add garlic and parsley to marinade; mix well. Let stand 2 hours or
   longer in marinade; serve calamari in marinade.

serves 4

per serving 19.3g fat; 986kJ
store Recipe can be made 2 days ahead and refrigerated, covered.

beans with tomato

PREPARATION TIME 35 MINUTES ■ COOKING TIME 40 MINUTES

30g butter

1 clove garlic, crushed

45g can anchovy fillets, drained, chopped finely

2 medium brown onions (300g), chopped finely

3 medium tomatoes (570g), chopped finely

1 tablespoon tomato paste

2 teaspoons finely chopped fresh basil

½ teaspoon sugar

1kg borlotti beans, shelled

1 cup (250ml) water

2 teaspoons finely shredded fresh basil, extra

1 Melt butter in large saucepan; cook garlic, anchovy, onion and tomato until onion is transparent. Add paste, basil, sugar and beans; mix until well combined.

2 Add the water; bring to a boil. Reduce heat; simmer, covered, about 30 minutes or until beans are tender. Stir through extra basil.

serves 6

per serving 8.2g fat; 2080kJ

tips 600g canned borlotti or cannellini beans can be substituted for the shelled borlotti beans; rinse and drain beans before adding for last 10 minutes of cooking.

Recipe can be made 2 days ahead and refrigerated, covered; reheat or bring to room temperature before serving.

roasted tomatoes
with garlic and herbs

PREPARATION TIME 10 MINUTES ■ COOKING TIME 1 HOUR

9 large egg tomatoes (1.2kg), halved

1 tablespoon extra virgin olive oil

1 teaspoon sea salt

1 teaspoon cracked black pepper

8 sprigs fresh thyme

2 cloves garlic, peeled, sliced thinly

2 teaspoons finely chopped fresh oregano

1 teaspoon finely chopped fresh thyme, extra

2 tablespoons extra virgin olive oil, extra

1 Place tomatoes in large baking dish with oil, salt, pepper, thyme and garlic.

2 Bake in moderately hot oven about 1 hour or until tender and browned lightly.

3 Drizzle with combined oregano, extra thyme and extra oil. Serve warm or cold.

serves 6

per serving 9.3g fat; 448kJ

store Recipe can be made 3 days ahead and refrigerated, covered.

carpaccio
with fresh herbs

PREPARATION TIME 25 MINUTES (plus freezing time)

500g piece of beef eye-fillet, about 6cm diameter
1/3 cup (80ml) extra virgin olive oil
1/4 cup (60ml) lemon juice
1/4 cup firmly packed fresh basil
1/4 cup firmly packed fresh flat-leaf parsley
1 tablespoon fresh oregano
1 tablespoon coarsely chopped fresh chives
1/4 cup (25g) drained sun-dried tomatoes, sliced thinly
2 tablespoons flaked parmesan cheese
freshly ground black pepper

1   Remove any excess fat from beef. Wrap beef tightly in plastic wrap; freeze about 1 1/2 hours or until partly frozen.

2   Cut beef into 1mm slices; freeze until required. *[Store in freezer container, between layers of freezer wrap, for up to 2 months.]*

3   Just before serving, place beef on serving plate. Drizzle with oil and juice; top with combined herbs, tomato, cheese and pepper.

serves 8

per serving 12.9g fat; 747kJ
tips Sashimi-quality tuna can be used in place of the beef; ask the fishmonger to slice tuna, paper-thin, for you.
Omit the parmesan and add a sprinkling of baby capers.

pesto dip
with crisp garlic wedges

PREPARATION TIME 10 MINUTES ■ COOKING TIME 25 MINUTES

1 cup firmly packed, coarsely chopped fresh basil

1 clove garlic, crushed

2 tablespoons pine nuts, toasted

2 tablespoons finely grated fresh parmesan cheese

2 tablespoons olive oil

2 teaspoons lemon juice

1¼ cups (300g) sour cream

crisp garlic wedges

4 pitta

150g butter, melted

2 cloves garlic, crushed

⅔ cup (50g) finely grated fresh parmesan cheese

1 Blend or process basil, garlic, pine nuts, cheese, oil and juice until smooth. Combine in medium bowl with sour cream.

2 Serve with crisp garlic wedges. *[Can be made a day ahead and refrigerated, covered.]*

crisp garlic wedges Split pitta in half; cut into large wedges. Place split-side up on oven trays. Brush with combined butter and garlic; sprinkle with cheese. Bake in moderately hot oven about 8 minutes or until browned lightly and crisp. *[Can be made a week ahead and stored in airtight container or frozen for up to 2 months.]*

serves 6

per serving 54.5g fat; 2696kJ

baked mushrooms

PREPARATION TIME 15 MINUTES ■ COOKING TIME 10 MINUTES

9 medium flat mushrooms (900g)

60g butter, melted

3 bacon rashers (210g), chopped finely

4 green onions, chopped finely

2 cloves garlic, crushed

2 tablespoons stale breadcrumbs

1 tablespoon cream

2 teaspoons fresh oregano, chopped coarsely

2 tablespoons grated parmesan cheese

1 Gently remove stalks from eight of the mushrooms. Finely chop stalks and remaining mushroom.

2 Brush mushroom caps all over with butter. Place on lightly greased oven trays.

3 Cook bacon and onion in small non-stick frying pan until bacon is crisp. Add chopped mushroom, garlic and breadcrumbs. Cook, stirring, until well combined. Remove from heat; stir in cream, oregano and cheese. Divide bacon mixture between mushroom caps. *[Can be made 3 hours ahead to this stage and refrigerated, covered.]*

4 Bake in moderately hot oven about 10 minutes or until hot.

serves 4

per serving 17.4g fat; 990kJ

tip Cap mushrooms can be substituted for the flat mushrooms. Cook 5 minutes; cool slightly before serving.

fennel vinaigrette

PREPARATION TIME 10 MINUTES ■ COOKING TIME 25 MINUTES

1^{1}/$_{2}$ **cups (375ml) water**
^{3}/$_{4}$ **cup (180ml) olive oil**
^{3}/$_{4}$ **cup (180ml) white vinegar**
^{1}/$_{4}$ **cup (60ml) dry white wine**
1 medium brown onion (150g), sliced thinly
1 clove garlic, crushed
8 whole black peppercorns
1 bay leaf
1^{1}/$_{2}$ **teaspoons yellow mustard seeds**
4 medium fennel bulbs (2kg)
1^{1}/$_{2}$ **tablespoons coarsely chopped fresh fennel leaves**

1 Combine the water, oil, vinegar, wine, onion, garlic, peppercorns, bay leaf and mustard seeds in large saucepan; bring to a boil. Reduce heat; simmer, uncovered, 4 minutes.

2 Trim tops from fennel bulbs; cut bulbs in half through centre. Add fennel halves to vinegar mixture in saucepan; bring to a boil. Reduce heat; simmer, covered, about 15 minutes or until just tender.

3 Remove fennel from liquid, taking off any remaining particles from fennel. Strain liquid into large bowl; add fennel halves. Cool; stir in fennel leaves.

serves 4

per serving 41.4g fat; 1911kJ
tip Recipe can be prepared 3 days ahead and refrigerated, covered.

marinated artichoke hearts

PREPARATION TIME 30 MINUTES (plus marinating and standing time) ■ COOKING TIME 20 MINUTES

10 medium globe artichokes (2kg)
3 medium lemons (420g), halved
1 clove garlic, crushed
1 teaspoon black peppercorns
1 litre (4 cups) white vinegar
2 cups (500ml) water
1½ cups (375ml) hot olive oil, approximately

1 Cut stems from artichokes. Snap off tough outer leaves until you are left with a central cone of leaves.

2 Trim away any dark green parts; cut away top of cones. Rub artichokes all over with a lemon half. Place artichokes in large non-reactive bowl with another lemon half; cover well with water.

3 Heat combined garlic, peppercorns, vinegar and the water in large non-reactive saucepan until hot; do not boil. Add drained artichokes and remaining lemons; simmer, uncovered, 15 minutes or until chokes are easy to remove from centres. Drain; cool 5 minutes.

4 Remove and discard centre leaves and chokes using a small spoon. Cut artichoke hearts in half; place hearts in sterilised 1-litre (4 cup) jar. Top with enough oil to cover, taking care as it will bubble. Leave 1cm space between hearts and top of jar; seal while hot. Refrigerate 1 week before using.

serves 8

per serving 7.3g fat; 445kJ
store Recipe can be made 3 months ahead and refrigerated.

baked mussels

24 small black mussels (500g)

¾ cup (180ml) water

¼ cup (60ml) olive oil

1 clove garlic, crushed

2 tablespoons finely chopped fresh parsley

½ cup (35g) stale breadcrumbs

1 medium tomato (130g), seeded, chopped finely

1 Scrub mussels, remove beards. Heat the water in large saucepan. Cook mussels in the water, covered, over high heat about 3 minutes or until shells open. Drain; discard liquid.

2 Loosen mussels; remove from shell. Discard half of each shell; reserve half. Combine mussel meat, oil, garlic, parsley and breadcrumbs in small bowl; mix well. Cover; refrigerate 30 minutes. *[Can be made a day ahead to this stage.]*

3 Place one mussel in each half shell; place on oven tray. Combine tomato with remaining breadcrumb mixture; spoon over mussels. Bake in hot oven about 5 minutes or until breadcrumbs are browned lightly.

serves 4

per serving 14.5g fat; 738kJ

olives in cheese pastry

PREPARATION TIME 35 MINUTES (plus refrigeration time)
COOKING TIME 20 MINUTES

1 cup (150g) plain flour
100g butter, chopped coarsely
1 cup (80g) finely grated parmesan cheese
2 teaspoons dried oregano
2 tablespoons water
50 small stuffed olives

1 Sift flour into a medium bowl; rub in butter. Stir in cheese and oregano; add enough of the water to make ingredients cling together. Cover; refrigerate 30 minutes.

2 Drain olives on absorbent paper.

3 Roll pastry between sheets of greaseproof paper until 3mm thick; cut 4cm rounds from pastry. Top each round with an olive; fold pastry around olive to enclose.

4 Place olives 1cm apart on greased oven trays. Cover; refrigerate 30 minutes. *[Can be made a day ahead to this stage.]*

5 Bake, uncovered, in moderately hot oven about 20 minutes or until golden; cool.

makes 50

per pastry 3.2g fat; 157kJ
store Recipe can be made a day ahead and stored in airtight container. Uncooked olives can be frozen for up to 3 months.
tip Pastry for wrapping olives is best rolled only once for the wrapping process – more rolling causes it to shrink on cooking.

orange and oregano marinated green olives

PREPARATION TIME 10 MINUTES (plus standing time)
COOKING TIME 5 MINUTES

600g large green olives, drained
3 orange slices, quartered
5 sprigs fresh oregano
1 cup (250ml) olive oil
½ cup (125ml) orange juice
2 teaspoons whole black pepper

1 Layer olives, orange and oregano into hot sterilised 1-litre (4 cup) jar.

2 Gently heat oil, juice and pepper in small saucepan. Pour enough of the oil mixture into jar to cover olives completely, leaving 1cm space between olives and top of jar; seal while hot.

makes 4 cups

per tablespoon 2.9g fat; 141kJ
store Recipe best made 3 days ahead; can be refrigerated 3 weeks.
tip Oil will solidify on refrigeration; bring to room temperature before serving.

black olive paste

4 cloves garlic, chopped coarsely
4 cups (480g) seeded black olives
5 anchovy fillets, drained
1/2 cup coarsely chopped fresh parsley
1 tablespoon coarsely chopped fresh oregano
1 tablespoon drained capers
1 cup (250ml) extra virgin olive oil

1 Blend or process garlic, olives, anchovy, parsley, oregano and capers until chopped finely.

2 Gradually add oil, in a thin stream, while motor is operating; process until smooth. Spoon into hot sterilised jar. Cover with a thin layer of oil; seal.

makes 3 1/2 cups

per tablespoon 8.3g fat; 355kJ
store Paste can be refrigerated 3 weeks.

garlic chilli black olives

750g black olives, drained
2 cups (500ml) olive oil
1/3 cup (80ml) balsamic vinegar
6 dried red thai chillies
4 cloves garlic, halved
3 strips lemon rind

1 Place olives in hot sterilised 1.25-litre (5 cup) jar.

2 Gently heat remaining ingredients in small saucepan until warm. Pour enough of the oil mixture into jar to cover olives completely, leaving 1cm space between olives and top of jar; seal while hot.

makes 5 cups

per tablespoon 2.5g fat; 150kJ
store Recipe best made 3 days ahead; can be refrigerated 3 weeks.

olives

soup

Hearty is probably the best word to describe Italian soups. Rich with a variety of vegetables, or fragrant with the abundant fresh seafood of the Mediterranean, finished with a sprinkling of grated parmesan or topped with freshly chopped herbs, these soups can often serve as meals in themselves. Just add crusty bread and a simple salad.

stracciatella

PREPARATION TIME 5 MINUTES ■ COOKING TIME 10 MINUTES

5 eggs

**½ cup (40g) finely grated
parmesan cheese**

1.5 litres (6 cups) chicken stock

**2 tablespoons finely chopped
fresh flat-leaf parsley**

ground nutmeg

1 Lightly whisk eggs with cheese in medium jug until combined.

2 Bring stock to a boil in large saucepan. Remove from heat; gradually add egg mixture, whisking constantly.

3 Return mixture to heat; simmer, stirring constantly, about 5 minutes or until egg mixture forms fine shreds. Stir in parsley; sprinkle with nutmeg.

serves 6

per serving 6.9g fat; 606kJ

tips Break eggs one at a time into a small cup before adding to the recipe; this way, if one egg is stale, you can discard it.

Make sure you add the egg and cheese mixture gradually or you will end up with large clumps of 'scrambled' egg.

seafood soup with gremolata

PREPARATION TIME 30 MINUTES ■ COOKING TIME 1 HOUR 20 MINUTES

2kg fish bones

1 medium brown onion (150g), chopped coarsely

1 medium carrot (120g), chopped coarsely

2 trimmed sticks celery (150g), chopped coarsely

4 litres (16 cups) water

8 black peppercorns

2 bay leaves

1 tablespoon olive oil

1 medium brown onion (150g), chopped coarsely, extra

2 cloves garlic, crushed

5 medium tomatoes (950g), chopped finely

3 teaspoons sugar

400g canned tomatoes

1/4 cup (70g) tomato paste

1/2 cup (125ml) dry white wine

2 medium uncooked lobster tails (760g), shelled, chopped coarsely

400g boneless firm white fish fillets, chopped coarsely

gremolata

1 clove garlic, chopped finely

1 tablespoon finely chopped lemon rind

2 tablespoons finely chopped fresh flat-leaf parsley

1 Combine fish bones, onion, carrot, celery, the water, peppercorns and bay leaves in large saucepan. Simmer, uncovered, 20 minutes. Strain stock over large bowl; discard bones, vegetables and seasonings. *[Can be made a day ahead to this stage and refrigerated, covered, or frozen for up to 2 months.]*

2 Heat oil in large saucepan; cook extra onion and garlic, stirring, until onion softens. Add tomato and sugar; cook, stirring, about 10 minutes or until tomato is soft. Stir in undrained crushed tomatoes, paste and wine; bring to a boil. Reduce heat; simmer, uncovered, about 5 minutes or until mixture thickens slightly, stirring occasionally. Add stock; bring to a boil. Reduce heat; simmer, uncovered, 20 minutes. Cool 10 minutes.

3 Blend or process tomato mixture, in batches, until pureed; return to cleaned saucepan. Bring to a boil; add lobster and fish. Reduce heat; simmer, stirring, about 5 minutes or until seafood is just cooked.

4 Divide soup among serving bowls; sprinkle each with gremolata.

gremolata Combine ingredients in small bowl.

serves 6

per serving 6.6g fat; 1232kJ

tip Prawns, crabs or yabbies can be substituted for the lobster.

rocket and pancetta soup

PREPARATION TIME 20 MINUTES ■ COOKING TIME 35 MINUTES

100g thinly sliced pancetta
1 tablespoon olive oil
1 medium red onion (170g), chopped coarsely
2 cloves garlic, quartered
1½ tablespoons balsamic vinegar
4 medium potatoes (800g), chopped coarsely
3 cups (750ml) chicken stock
3 cups (750ml) water
500g rocket, trimmed
¼ cup (20g) finely grated parmesan cheese

1 Place pancetta in single layer on oven tray. Bake, uncovered, in moderate oven, about 15 minutes or until crisp. Drain pancetta on absorbent paper; chop coarsely.

2 Heat oil in large saucepan; cook onion and garlic, stirring, until onion softens. Add vinegar and potato; cook, stirring, 5 minutes.

3 Add stock and the water; bring to a boil. Reduce heat; simmer, uncovered, about 15 minutes or until potato softens. Stir in rocket; cook, stirring, about 2 minutes or until rocket wilts.

4 Blend or process soup mixture, in batches, until smooth. Return soup to cleaned saucepan; stir over heat until hot. Divide soup among serving bowls; sprinkle with cheese and pancetta.

serves 6

per serving 7g fat; 855kJ
tip Prosciutto can be substituted for the pancetta.

tuscan bean soup

PREPARATION TIME 25 MINUTES (plus soaking and standing time) ■ COOKING TIME 1 HOUR 40 MINUTES

1¹/₂ cups (300g) dried haricot beans

1 tablespoon olive oil

1 medium brown onion (150g), chopped coarsely

2 cloves garlic, crushed

2 trimmed sticks celery (150g), chopped coarsely

1 medium carrot (120g), chopped coarsely

2 bacon rashers (140g), chopped coarsely

4 large ripe tomatoes (1kg), peeled, chopped coarsely

1.5 litres (6 cups) vegetable stock

1 teaspoon sugar

¹/₄ cup fresh parsley sprigs

¹/₄ cup (70g) tomato paste

1 Cover beans with water in large bowl; stand, covered, overnight.

2 Heat oil in large saucepan; cook onion, garlic, celery, carrot and bacon, stirring, until vegetables are just tender.

3 Add tomato; cook, stirring, about 5 minutes or until tomato is soft.

4 Stir in rinsed drained beans, stock, sugar, parsley and paste; bring to a boil. Reduce heat; simmer, covered, about 1¹/₂ hours or until beans are tender. *[Can be made a day ahead and refrigerated, covered or frozen for up to 2 months.]*

serves 4

per serving 16.8g fat; 3060kJ

minestrone

PREPARATION TIME 25 MINUTES (plus soaking time) ■ COOKING TIME 1 HOUR 10 MINUTES

½ cup (100g) dried cannellini beans

2 teaspoons olive oil

1 medium brown onion (150g), chopped finely

2 cloves garlic, crushed

10 slices prosciutto (150g), chopped coarsely

1 trimmed stick celery (75g), chopped finely

1 medium carrot (120g), chopped finely

1 medium green zucchini (120g), chopped finely

800g canned tomatoes

1.5 litres (6 cups) chicken stock

1 medium potato (200g), chopped finely

1 cup (170g) ditalini

1 cup (80g) loosely packed finely shredded savoy cabbage

1 cup loosely packed, finely shredded spinach leaves

1 tablespoon finely shredded fresh basil

½ cup (40g) grated parmesan cheese

1 Place beans in medium bowl; cover with water. Stand overnight; drain.

2 Heat oil in large saucepan; cook onion and garlic, stirring, until onion is soft. Add prosciutto, celery, carrot and zucchini; cook, stirring, 5 minutes. Stir in undrained crushed tomatoes and stock; bring to a boil. Reduce heat; simmer, uncovered, 30 minutes.

3 Stir in beans and potato; simmer, uncovered, 15 minutes. *[Can be made a day ahead to this stage and refrigerated, covered, or frozen for up to 3 months.]*

4 Add pasta; simmer, uncovered, about 10 minutes or until pasta is tender.

5 Just before serving, stir in cabbage, spinach and basil; serve soup sprinkled with cheese.

serves 6

per serving 8.7g fat; 1472kJ

tips Macaroni or any small tubular pasta can be substituted for the ditalini.
Make basic soup mixture (up to and including step 3) when you soak the beans (ie, the day before required), to allow the flavours to develop. Top each bowl of soup with a teaspoon of basil pesto, to make minestrone genovese.

lentil soup

PREPARATION TIME 15 MINUTES ■ COOKING TIME 1 HOUR 25 MINUTES

¼ cup (60ml) olive oil
1 large brown onion (200g), chopped coarsely
1 medium eggplant (300g), quartered
4 medium tomatoes (760g), quartered
1 large red capsicum (350g), quartered
3 cloves garlic, peeled
2 litres (8 cups) vegetable stock
1 cup (200g) puy lentils
½ cup (125ml) sour cream
2 tablespoons finely chopped fresh chives

1 Combine oil, onion, eggplant, tomato, capsicum and garlic in large baking dish. Bake, uncovered, in hot oven about 45 minutes or until vegetables are tender. Turn once halfway through cooking.

2 Place capsicum pieces on plate, skin-side up. Cover; stand 5 minutes. Peel capsicum, tomato and eggplant; discard skin. Chop flesh coarsely keeping each vegetable separate.

3 Blend or process eggplant with garlic and onion until pureed; combine with stock and lentils in large saucepan. Bring to a boil; reduce heat; simmer, uncovered, about 35 minutes or until lentils are tender. *[Can be made a day ahead to this stage and refrigerated, covered.]*

4 Add capsicum and tomato; stir over heat until hot. Divide soup among serving bowls. Dollop each with sour cream; sprinkle with chives.

serves 6

per serving 19.2g fat; 1409kJ
tip Brown lentils can be substituted for the puy lentils, although they do require longer cooking.

olive bread with oregano

PREPARATION TIME 25 MINUTES (plus standing time)
COOKING TIME 45 MINUTES (plus cooling time)

1 tablespoon dry yeast
1 teaspoon sugar
2¼ cups (560ml) skim milk
5½ cups (825g) plain flour
⅓ cup (80ml) olive oil
1¼ cups (150g) seeded black olives, halved
2 tablespoons coarsely chopped fresh oregano

1 Combine yeast, sugar and milk in large bowl; stir in 3 cups (450g) of the flour. Cover; stand in warm place 30 minutes or until foamy. Stir in oil, then remaining flour. Knead on floured surface about 10 minutes or until smooth and elastic. Place dough in large oiled bowl. Cover; stand in warm place until doubled in size.

2 Meanwhile, drain olives on absorbent paper.

3 Turn dough onto floured surface; knead in olives and oregano. Roll dough into 30cm x 35cm oval; fold almost in half. Place on large greased oven tray; sift 2 tablespoons of plain flour over dough.

4 Bake, uncovered, in moderately hot oven 45 minutes or until cooked when tested; cool on wire rack.

serves 10

per serving 8.5g fat; 1632kJ
store Bread can be made a day ahead and warmed before serving. Store in airtight container.

pagnotta

PREPARATION TIME 25 MINUTES (plus standing time)
COOKING TIME 40 MINUTES (plus cooling time)

2 teaspoons dry yeast
½ teaspoon sugar
2 teaspoons salt
3½ cups (525g) plain flour
1¼ cups (310ml) skim milk, warmed
1 tablespoon olive oil

1 Combine yeast, sugar, salt and flour in large bowl. Gradually stir in milk and half of the oil until combined.

2 Knead dough on lightly floured surface about 2 minutes or until well combined. Place dough in large oiled bowl; turn to coat in oil. Cover; stand in warm place about 30 minutes or until dough doubles in size.

3 Turn dough onto floured surface; knead 10 minutes or until dough is smooth and elastic. Shape dough into 58cm log; place on an oiled and floured oven tray. Lightly brush ends with water; gently press together to form a ring. Combine remaining oil and 2 teaspoons warm water in small bowl; brush over dough. Sift over a little extra plain flour.

4 Place in cold oven; turn temperature to moderately hot. Bake, uncovered, about 40 minutes or until cooked when tested; cool on wire rack.

serves 6

per serving 4.2g fat; 1471kJ

onion focaccia

PREPARATION TIME 20 MINUTES (plus standing time)
COOKING TIME 25 MINUTES (plus cooling time)

- 2½ cups (375g) plain flour
- 2 teaspoons (7g) dry yeast
- ¼ cup (20g) grated parmesan cheese
- 2 tablespoons coarsely chopped fresh sage
- 3 teaspoons sea salt flakes
- 1 cup (250ml) warm water
- ¼ cup (60ml) olive oil
- 1 small white onion (80g), sliced thinly

1 Sift flour in large bowl; stir in yeast, cheese, sage and 1 teaspoon of the salt. Gradually stir in the water and 2 tablespoons of the oil. Knead on well floured surface about 10 minutes or until smooth and elastic.

2 Place on greased oven tray; press into a 24cm-round. Cover with greased plastic wrap; stand in warm place until dough doubles in size.

3 Meanwhile combine onion, remaining salt and remaining oil in small bowl. Remove plastic wrap from dough; sprinkle dough with onion mixture. Bake, uncovered, in hot oven about 25 minutes or until cooked when tested; cool on wire rack.

serves 8

per serving 8.2g fat; 999kJ

cheese breadsticks

PREPARATION TIME 30 MINUTES (plus standing time)
COOKING TIME 10 MINUTES (plus cooling time)

- 60g butter, melted
- 1 teaspoon dry yeast
- 2 tablespoons olive oil
- 2 teaspoons sugar
- ½ teaspoon salt
- 1¼ cups (100g) grated parmesan cheese
- ¾ cup warm water (180ml)
- 2½ cups (375g) plain flour

1 Combine butter, yeast, oil, sugar, salt, cheese and the water in large bowl; gradually stir in flour. Knead on lightly floured surface about 10 minutes or until smooth and elastic. Place dough in large oiled bowl; turn to coat in oil. Stand in warm place 10 minutes.

2 Cut dough into quarters; roll each quarter into 10 logs, about 20cm long. Place 1cm apart on lightly greased oven trays.

3 Bake, uncovered, in hot oven about 20 minutes or until crisp and browned; cool on wire racks.

makes 40

per breadstick 3.1g fat; 266kJ
store Breadsticks can be kept in an airtight container 2 weeks.

bread

pasta

For many centuries, the Italian people have embraced pasta with fervour, giving it something of the status of a national dish. The result is a wealth of delicious recipes as varied as the shapes of pasta itself – sometimes rich and hearty, sometimes creamy and delicate, but always easy to prepare and popular with adults and children alike.

pappardelle
with chilli and semi-dried tomato sauce

PREPARATION TIME 15 MINUTES ■ COOKING TIME 25 MINUTES

2 medium brown onions (300g), chopped coarsely

2 cloves garlic, quartered

1 cup (150g) semi-dried tomatoes in oil, drained

¼ cup (70g) tomato paste

2 fresh red thai chillies, seeded, chopped finely

2 cups (500ml) beef stock

375g pappardelle

¼ cup coarsely chopped fresh flat-leaf parsley

freshly ground black pepper

1 Blend or process onion, garlic, tomatoes, tomato paste and chilli until mixture forms a paste.

2 Heat large non-stick frying pan; cook tomato mixture, stirring, 10 minutes. Stir in stock; bring to a boil. Reduce heat; simmer sauce, uncovered, about 10 minutes or until thickened slightly. *[Can be made 2 days ahead to this stage and refrigerated, covered, or frozen for up to 6 months.]*

3 Meanwhile, cook pasta in large saucepan of boiling water, uncovered, until just tender; drain.

4 Just before serving, gently toss pasta through sauce; sprinkle with parsley and pepper.

serves 6

per serving 2.9g fat; 1147kJ

tip Pappardelle is the widest ribbon pasta available; any long pasta such as fettuccine or tagliatelle can be substituted.

spaghetti marinara

PREPARATION TIME 5 MINUTES ■ COOKING TIME 15 MINUTES

1 tablespoon olive oil

1 medium brown onion (150g), chopped finely

1/3 cup (80ml) dry white wine

1/3 cup (95g) tomato paste

850g canned tomatoes

750g seafood marinara mix

1/4 cup loosely packed, coarsely chopped fresh flat-leaf parsley

375g spaghetti

1 Heat oil in large frying pan; cook onion, stirring, until soft.

2 Add wine, paste and undrained crushed tomatoes to pan; bring to a boil. Reduce heat; simmer, uncovered, 10 minutes or until sauce thickens slightly.

3 Add marinara mix; cook, stirring occasionally, about 5 minutes or until seafood is cooked through. Stir in parsley.

4 Meanwhile, cook pasta in large saucepan of boiling water, uncovered, until just tender; drain.

5 Serve marinara over pasta.

serves 4

per serving 11.6g fat; 2820kJ

lasagne

1 tablespoon olive oil

1 medium onion (150g), chopped finely

1 medium carrot (120g), chopped finely

1 trimmed stick celery (75g), chopped finely

2 cloves garlic, crushed

500g minced beef

1/3 cup (80ml) dry red wine

850g canned tomatoes

2 tablespoons tomato paste

1/2 cup (125ml) water

4 slices prosciutto (60g), chopped finely

1 tablespoon coarsely chopped fresh oregano

2 tablespoons coarsely chopped fresh parsley

18 instant lasagne sheets

1/2 cup (40g) grated parmesan cheese

cheese sauce

60g butter

1/3 cup (50g) plain flour

1 litre (4 cups) milk

3/4 cup (60g) grated parmesan cheese

pinch ground nutmeg

1 Heat oil in large frying pan; cook onion, carrot, celery and garlic, stirring, until onion is soft. Add beef; cook, stirring, until browned. Add wine; bring to a boil. Stir in undrained crushed tomatoes, paste and the water; reduce heat. Simmer, uncovered, about 1 hour or until mixture is thick. Stir in prosciutto and herbs; cool slightly.

2 Place six lasagne sheets into greased shallow 3-litre (12 cup) ovenproof dish. Spread with half of the meat sauce; drizzle with 1 cup (250ml) of the cheese sauce. Repeat layers again.

3 Top with remaining pasta sheets. Spread with remaining cheese sauce; sprinkle with cheese. Bake in moderate oven about 45 minutes or until pasta is tender and lasagne is browned.

cheese sauce Heat butter in large saucepan; cook flour, stirring over heat until flour bubbles and thickens. Remove from heat; gradually stir in milk. Cook, until mixture boils and thickens. Remove from heat; stir in cheese and nutmeg. Cool 10 minutes.

serves 6

per serving 32.4g fat; 2934kJ

store Recipe best made a day ahead; can be made 3 days ahead and refrigerated, covered, or frozen for up to 2 months.

cheese and spinach tortellini with
gorgonzola sauce

PREPARATION TIME 5 MINUTES ■ COOKING TIME 15 MINUTES

30g butter

2 tablespoons plain flour

1 cup (250ml) milk

3/4 cup (180ml) cream

100g gorgonzola cheese, chopped coarsely

750g cheese and spinach tortellini

1/4 cup loosely packed fresh flat-leaf parsley

freshly ground black pepper

1 Melt butter in medium saucepan; cook flour, stirring, about 2 minutes or until mixture bubbles and thickens.

2 Gradually stir in milk and cream; bring to a boil. Reduce heat; simmer, uncovered, until sauce boils and thickens. Remove from heat; stir in cheese.

3 Meanwhile, cook pasta in large saucepan of boiling water, uncovered, until just tender; drain.

4 Combine pasta with sauce; sprinkle with parsley and pepper.

serves 4

per serving 43.8g fat; 3017kJ

tips Ravioli or gnocchi can be substituted for the tortellini.

It's best to choose a ricotta-and-spinach-filled tortellini (or the even simpler ricotta-filled version) when making this sauce, as it doesn't marry overly well with meat-filled pastas.

rigatoni with eggplant sauce

PREPARATION TIME 10 MINUTES ■ COOKING TIME 20 MINUTES

¼ cup (60ml) olive oil

1 medium brown onion (150g), chopped finely

2 trimmed sticks celery (150g), chopped finely

1 clove garlic, crushed

2 tablespoons brandy

1 medium eggplant (300g), sliced thinly

2⅓ cups (580ml) bottled tomato pasta sauce

½ cup (140g) tomato paste

½ cup (125ml) water

375g rigatoni

¼ cup (20g) finely grated parmesan cheese

1 Heat oil in large saucepan; cook onion, celery and garlic, stirring, until onion softens. Add brandy; cook, stirring, until brandy evaporates. Add eggplant; cook, stirring, until eggplant is tender.

2 Stir in sauce, paste and the water; bring to a boil. Reduce heat; simmer, uncovered, about 10 minutes or until sauce thickens slightly. *[Can be made 2 days ahead to this stage and refrigerated, covered.]*

3 Meanwhile, cook pasta in large saucepan of boiling water, uncovered, until just tender; drain. Place pasta in large warmed bowl with half of the eggplant sauce; toss gently to combine. Divide pasta among serving plates; top each with remaining sauce. Serve with cheese.

serves 4

per serving 16.9g fat; 2420kJ

tip Before serving, warm large bowls and platters, by placing in a sink of very hot water 10 minutes; dry before using.

spaghetti with herbed ricotta

PREPARATION TIME 10 MINUTES ■ COOKING TIME 15 MINUTES

500g spaghetti
450g fresh ricotta
3 egg yolks
3/4 cup (180ml) milk
1/3 cup firmly packed, coarsely chopped fresh flat-leaf parsley
1/4 cup firmly packed, coarsely chopped fresh basil
3 green onions, chopped finely
2 cloves garlic, crushed
1/4 cup (20g) finely grated pepato cheese
freshly ground black pepper

1 Cook pasta in large saucepan of boiling water, uncovered, until just tender; drain.

2 Whisk ricotta, yolks and milk in large bowl until smooth; stir in herbs, onion, garlic and cheese.

3 Add pasta to ricotta mixture; toss gently to combine. Sprinkle with pepper to serve.

serves 4

per serving 21.7g fat; 2863kJ

tips Pepato can be substituted with another hard cheese, such as romano or an aged provolone.

Feel free to use other herbs, such as chives or oregano, instead of the basil.

fettuccine carbonara

PREPARATION TIME 10 MINUTES ■ COOKING TIME 10 MINUTES

**4 bacon rashers (280g),
chopped coarsely**

375g fettuccine

3 egg yolks, beaten

1 cup (250ml) cream

**½ cup (40g) finely grated
parmesan cheese**

**2 tablespoons coarsely chopped
fresh chives**

1 Cook bacon in small heated frying pan, stirring, until crisp; drain.

2 Just before serving, cook pasta in large saucepan of boiling water, uncovered, until just tender; drain.

3 Combine pasta in warmed large bowl with yolks, cream and cheese; sprinkle with chives and freshly ground black pepper, if desired.

serves 4

per serving 42g fat; 3222kJ

tip Pancetta or prosciutto can be substituted for the bacon, and grated romano or pepato can be substituted for the parmesan.

fettuccine with meatballs
in rosemary paprika sauce

PREPARATION TIME 15 MINUTES ■ COOKING TIME 45 MINUTES

250g lean minced beef

½ cup (35g) stale breadcrumbs

**1 tablespoon finely chopped
fresh parsley**

**1 tablespoon finely chopped
fresh chives**

1 egg white

1 teaspoon worcestershire sauce

2 teaspoons olive oil

250g fettuccine

rosemary paprika sauce

425g canned tomatoes

1 cup (250ml) water

2 tablespoons dry red wine

**1 medium brown onion (150g),
chopped finely**

½ teaspoon worcestershire sauce

1 teaspoon sweet paprika

3 sprigs rosemary

1 Combine beef, breadcrumbs, parsley, chives, egg white and sauce in large bowl. Shape mixture into small meatballs.

2 Heat oil in medium non-stick saucepan; cook meatballs until well browned all over and cooked through. Drain on absorbent paper.

3 Meanwhile, cook pasta in large saucepan of boiling water until tender; drain.

4 Add meatballs to rosemary paprika sauce; mix well. Stir until heated through. *[Can be made 2 days ahead to this stage and refrigerated, covered, or frozen for up to 3 months.]*

5 Serve pasta with meatballs in rosemary paprika sauce.

rosemary paprika sauce Combine undrained crushed tomatoes with remaining ingredients in medium saucepan; bring to a boil. Reduce heat; simmer, uncovered, about 20 minutes or until thickened slightly.

serves 2

per serving 15.8g fat; 3303kJ

chicken and prosciutto cannelloni

50g butter

1/4 cup (35g) plain flour

2/3 cup (160ml) milk

1 1/2 cups (375ml) chicken stock

**1/2 cup (40g) finely grated
parmesan cheese**

**400g fontina cheese,
grated coarsely**

1 tablespoon olive oil

**2 medium brown onions (300g),
chopped finely**

3 cloves garlic, crushed

1 kg chicken mince

**2 tablespoons finely chopped
fresh sage**

850g canned tomatoes

1/2 cup (125ml) dry white wine

1/4 cup (70g) tomato paste

3 teaspoons sugar

12 fresh lasagne sheets

24 slices prosciutto (360g)

1 Heat butter in medium saucepan; cook flour, stirring, until flour thickens and bubbles. Gradually stir in milk and stock; cook, stirring, until sauce boils and thickens. Remove from heat; stir in parmesan and a quarter of the fontina.

2 Heat oil in large saucepan; cook onion and garlic, stirring, until onion is soft. Add chicken; cook, stirring, until browned. Stir in sage. Combine chicken and cheese sauce in large bowl; cool.

3 Combine undrained crushed tomatoes, wine, paste and sugar in same large pan; cook, stirring, 10 minutes. Cool 10 minutes; blend or process, in batches, until smooth.

4 Cut pasta sheets and prosciutto slices in half crossways. Place two pieces of prosciutto on each piece of pasta. Top each with 1/4 cup chicken mixture; roll to enclose filling. Repeat with remaining pasta, prosciutto and chicken mixture.

5 Oil two 3-litre (12 cup) ovenproof dishes. Pour a quarter of the tomato sauce into base of each prepared dish; place half of the pasta rolls, seam-side down, in each dish. Pour remaining tomato sauce over rolls; sprinkle each dish with remaining fontina. *[Can be made 2 days ahead to this stage and refrigerated, covered, or frozen for up to 2 months.]*

6 Bake cannelloni, covered, in moderate oven 30 minutes. Uncover, bake further 15 minutes or until cheese melts and browns. Serve with a green salad, if desired.

serves 8

per serving 40.3g fat; 2998kJ

tip Pancetta or double-smoked ham can be substituted for the prosciutto.

bow ties and salmon in lemon cream

PREPARATION TIME 10 MINUTES ■ COOKING TIME 15 MINUTES

375g bow ties pasta

1 medium lemon (140g)

415g canned red salmon, drained, flaked

½ cup (125ml) cream

4 green onions, sliced thinly

1 Cook pasta in large saucepan of boiling water, uncovered, until just tender; drain.

2 Meanwhile, using zester, remove rind from lemon. Place rind and pasta in large saucepan with salmon, cream and onion; stir over low heat until hot.

serves 4

per serving 24.7g fat; 2524kJ

pasta primavera

PREPARATION TIME 15 MINUTES ■ COOKING TIME 15 MINUTES

375g small spiral pasta

1 tablespoon olive oil

1 medium brown onion (150g), chopped finely

3 cloves garlic, crushed

300g yellow patty-pan squash, quartered

1 medium red capsicum (200g), sliced thinly

200g sugar snap peas

1 medium carrot (120g), cut into ribbons

1¼ cups (310ml) cream

1 tablespoon seeded mustard

2 tablespoons finely chopped fresh flat-leaf parsley

1 Cook pasta in large saucepan of boiling water, uncovered, until just tender; drain.

2 Meanwhile, heat oil in large saucepan; cook onion and garlic, stirring, until onion softens. Add squash; cook, stirring, until just tender. Add capsicum, peas and carrot; cook, stirring, until capsicum is just tender.

3 Place pasta in pan with vegetables; add combined remaining ingredients. Stir over low heat until just hot.

serves 4

per serving 38.9g fat; 3033kJ

spaghetti puttanesca

PREPARATION TIME 15 MINUTES ■ COOKING TIME 20 MINUTES

¼ cup (60ml) olive oil
2 cloves garlic, crushed
4 medium tomatoes (760g), chopped coarsely
½ cup finely chopped fresh parsley
12 stuffed olives, sliced thinly
45g canned anchovy fillets, chopped finely
1 tablespoon finely chopped fresh basil
pinch chilli powder
375g spaghetti

1 Heat oil in medium saucepan; cook garlic until just changed in colour.

2 Add tomato, parsley, olives, anchovy, basil and chilli powder; cook further 3 minutes.

3 Meanwhile, cook pasta in large saucepan of boiling water, uncovered, until just tender; drain.

4 Combine pasta in large warmed bowl, with sauce; toss gently.

serves 4

per serving 16.9g fat; 2055kJ

spaghetti with pesto

PREPARATION TIME 15 MINUTES ■ COOKING TIME 15 MINUTES

2 cups coarsely chopped fresh basil

2 tablespoons pine nuts, toasted

2 cloves garlic

1/3 cup (80ml) olive oil

1/4 cup (20g) finely grated parmesan cheese

375g spaghetti

1 Blend or process basil, pine nuts and garlic until smooth. With processor operating, add oil in thin stream; process further 1 second.

2 Place basil mixture in medium bowl. Add cheese; mix until combined.

3 Cook pasta in large saucepan of boiling water, uncovered, until just tender; drain.

4 Combine pasta with pesto in large warmed bowl; toss gently.

serves 4

per serving 26.5 fat; 2363kJ

store Pesto can be made 2 weeks ahead and refrigerated in sterilised jar with a thin layer of olive oil over top, or frozen, in freezer container, for up to 3 months.

ricotta and silverbeet lasagne

PREPARATION TIME 15 MINUTES ■ COOKING TIME 1 HOUR 5 MINUTES

1kg silverbeet, trimmed

3 eggs, beaten lightly

2 cups (400g) ricotta cheese

¼ cup (20g) coarsely grated parmesan cheese

3 green onions, chopped finely

1½ cups (375ml) bottled tomato pasta sauce

12 sheets instant lasagne

1 cup (120g) coarsely grated cheddar cheese

1 Boil, steam or microwave silverbeet until just wilted; drain. Squeeze as much liquid as possible from silverbeet; chop coarsely. Combine egg, ricotta, parmesan and onion in large bowl; stir in silverbeet.

2 Spread half of the pasta sauce over base of oiled shallow baking dish. Cover with three sheets lasagne; top with a third of the silverbeet mixture. Cover silverbeet layer with three sheets of the lasagne; repeat layering with remaining silverbeet mixture and remaining lasagne sheets. Top lasagne with remaining pasta sauce; sprinkle with cheddar.

3 Cover lasagne with foil; bake in moderate oven 40 minutes. *[Can be made 2 days ahead to this stage and refrigerated, covered, or frozen for up to 3 months.]*

4 Remove foil; bake 20 minutes or until browned on top.

serves 4

per serving 28.4g fat; 2394kJ

fettuccine boscaiola

PREPARATION TIME 10 MINUTES ■ COOKING TIME 20 MINUTES

2 teaspoons olive oil

**200g button mushrooms,
  sliced thickly**

2 cloves garlic, crushed

200g shaved ham, chopped coarsely

1/4 cup (60ml) dry white wine

1 1/4 cups (310ml) cream

500g fettuccine

**2 tablespoons coarsely chopped
  fresh chives**

1 Heat oil in large saucepan; cook mushrooms, garlic and ham, stirring, until ingredients are browned lightly. Add wine; boil, uncovered, until wine reduces by half.

2 Add cream to mushroom mixture; reduce heat. Simmer, uncovered, until sauce thickens slightly.

3 Meanwhile, cook pasta in large saucepan of boiling water, uncovered, until just tender; drain.

4 Add chives and pasta to sauce; toss gently until mixed well.

serves 4

per serving 32.6g fat; 3294kJ

chicken ravioli with tarragon sauce

PREPARATION TIME 25 MINUTES (plus refrigeration time) ■ COOKING TIME 30 MINUTES

750g chicken mince

2 green onions, sliced thinly

**2 teaspoons finely grated
   lemon rind**

56 gow gee wrappers

1 egg, beaten lightly

2 teaspoons olive oil

**1 medium brown onion (150g),
   chopped finely**

2 cloves garlic, crushed

½ cup (125ml) dry white wine

1 tablespoon dijon mustard

2⅓ cups (580ml) cream

**2 tablespoons shredded fresh
   tarragon leaves**

1 Combine chicken, green onion and rind in medium bowl.

2 Brush one wrapper at a time with egg. Place a rounded teaspoon of the chicken mixture in centre of wrapper. Fold over to enclose filling; press edge to seal. Repeat with remaining wrappers, egg and chicken mixture. Place ravioli, in single layer, on tray. Cover; refrigerate 30 minutes. *[Can be made ahead to this stage and frozen for up to 2 months.]*

3 Heat oil in medium saucepan; cook brown onion and garlic, stirring, until onion is just browned. Add wine; cook, stirring, about 5 minutes or until wine reduces by a half. Stir in mustard and cream; cook sauce, stirring, until mixture just boils.

4 Meanwhile, cook ravioli, uncovered, in large saucepan of boiling water until each ravioli floats to the top. Remove ravioli with slotted spoon; drain. Return ravioli to pan; add tarragon and cream sauce. Toss gently until warmed through.

serves 8

per serving 38.5g fat; 2233kJ

fettuccine alfredo

PREPARATION TIME 5 MINUTES ■ COOKING TIME 15 MINUTES

375g fettuccine

90g butter, chopped coarsely

²/₃ cup (150ml) cream

1 cup (80g) finely grated parmesan cheese

2 tablespoons finely chopped fresh flat-leaf parsley

1 Cook pasta in large saucepan of boiling water, uncovered, until just tender; drain. Keep pasta warm while preparing sauce.

2 Place butter and cream in medium saucepan. Stir over low heat until butter melts and combines well with cream; remove from heat. Add cheese; stir until sauce is blended and smooth.

3 Spoon sauce over hot pasta; toss well. Serve sprinkled with parsley.

serves 4

per serving 42.3g fat; 2997kJ

spaghetti bolognese

PREPARATION TIME 15 MINUTES ■ COOKING TIME 2 HOURS 15 MINUTES

2 tablespoons olive oil
1 large brown onion (200g), chopped finely
750g minced beef
425g canned tomatoes
1 teaspoon fresh basil
1 teaspoon fresh oregano
1/2 teaspoon fresh thyme
1/3 cup (95g) tomato paste
1 litre (4 cups) water
250g spaghetti
grated parmesan cheese

1 Heat oil in large saucepan; cook onion until golden brown. Add beef to pan; cook until beef browns, mashing with fork occasionally to break up lumps. Pour off any surplus fat.

2 Push undrained tomatoes through sieve; add to pan. Add herbs, paste and the water; bring to a boil. Reduce heat; simmer, very gently, uncovered, about 1 1/2 hours, or until nearly all liquid evaporates. *[Can be made 2 days ahead to this stage and refrigerated, covered, or frozen for up to 3 months.]*

3 Cook spaghetti in large saucepan of boiling water until just tender; drain well.

4 Arrange hot spaghetti in individual serving bowls; top with sauce. Sprinkle with cheese.

serves 4

per serving 28.7g fat; 1867kJ

tip A true bolognese sauce contains no garlic, however two crushed cloves of garlic can be added to the tomatoes in step 2, if desired.

pagli e fieno

PREPARATION TIME 10 MINUTES ■ COOKING TIME 15 MINUTES

2 teaspoons olive oil

5 green onions, sliced thinly

2 cloves garlic, crushed

500g button mushrooms, sliced thickly

1 tablespoon dry white wine

1¼ cups (310ml) cream

¼ cup coarsely chopped fresh flat-leaf parsley

150g plain fettuccine

150g spinach-flavoured fettuccine

1 Heat oil in medium saucepan; cook onion and garlic, stirring, until onion softens.

2 Add mushrooms; cook, stirring, until just browned. Add wine and cream; bring to a boil. Reduce heat; simmer, uncovered, about 5 minutes or until sauce thickens slightly. Stir in parsley.

3 Meanwhile, cook both pastas in large saucepan of boiling water, uncovered, until just tender; drain. Place pasta in large warmed bowl with sauce; toss gently to combine.

serves 4

per serving 36g fat; 2339kJ

penne arrabiata

PREPARATION TIME 10 MINUTES ■ COOKING TIME 15 MINUTES

1 tablespoon olive oil

2 medium brown onions (300g), chopped finely

5 cloves garlic, crushed

3 fresh red thai chillies, chopped finely

2¹/₃ cups (580ml) bottled tomato pasta sauce

2 teaspoons balsamic vinegar

375g penne

¹/₄ cup (20g) finely grated parmesan cheese

1   Heat oil in large saucepan; cook onion, garlic and chilli, stirring, until onion softens. Add sauce and vinegar; bring to a boil. Reduce heat; simmer, uncovered, about 5 minutes or until sauce thickens slightly. *[Can be made a day ahead to this stage and refrigerated, covered, or frozen for up to 6 months.]*

2   Meanwhile, cook pasta in large saucepan of boiling water, uncovered, until just tender; drain. Combine pasta with sauce; sprinkle with cheese.

serves 4

per serving   7.6g fat; 1904kJ

tip   Leftover pasta and sauce can be placed in an oiled ovenproof dish, covered with mozzarella and baked in moderate oven until heated through and cheese bubbles.

spaghetti napoletana

PREPARATION TIME 5 MINUTES ■ COOKING TIME 25 MINUTES

2 teaspoons olive oil

1 small brown onion (80g), chopped finely

3 cloves garlic, crushed

850g canned tomatoes

1/4 cup coarsely chopped, firmly packed fresh basil

1/3 cup coarsely chopped, firmly packed fresh flat-leaf parsley

375g spaghetti

1 Heat oil in large saucepan; cook onion and garlic, stirring, until onion softens.

2 Add undrained crushed tomatoes; bring to a boil. Reduce heat; simmer, uncovered, about 20 minutes or until reduced by about a third. Stir in basil and parsley. *[Can be made a day ahead to this stage and refrigerated, covered, or frozen for up to 3 months.]*

3 Meanwhile, cook pasta in large saucepan of boiling water, uncovered, until just tender; drain. Serve pasta topped with sauce.

serves 4

per serving 4g fat; 1666kJ

tip If you cook this sauce even longer, until it reduces by half, it makes a good pizza-base sauce or, with capers stirred through it, a delicious topping for chicken or veal scaloppine.

roasted capsicum and prosciutto bruschetta

PREPARATION TIME 20 MINUTES
COOKING TIME 7 MINUTES

½ loaf ciabatta (275g)
3 cloves garlic, halved
¼ cup (60ml) olive oil
2 medium red capsicums (400g)
5 prosciutto slices (75g), chopped coarsely
1 tablespoon balsamic vinegar
2 tablespoons fresh oregano

1 Cut ciabatta into 1.5cm thick slices; halve any large slices crossways. Toast under hot grill until browned lightly; while still hot, rub one side of toast with garlic. Place toast in single layer on tray; drizzle oil evenly over toast. *[Can be made 3 hours ahead to this stage and covered.]*

2 Quarter capsicums; remove and discard seeds and membranes. Place capsicum on oven tray; roast under hot grill or in very hot oven, skin-side up, until skin blisters and blackens. Cover capsicum pieces in plastic 5 minutes. Peel away skin; discard. Cut capsicum into thin strips.

3 Cook prosciutto in medium heated non-stick frying pan until crisp. Add capsicum and vinegar to pan; stir to combine. Cool to room temperature.

4 Just before serving divide capsicum mixture among bruschetta; top with oregano.

serves 8

per serving 8.4g fat; 695kJ

bruschetta with creamy mushrooms

PREPARATION TIME 20 MINUTES
COOKING TIME 15 MINUTES

½ loaf ciabatta (275g)
4 cloves garlic, halved
½ cup (125ml) olive oil
250g flat mushrooms, chopped finely
1 tablespoon lemon juice
½ cup (125ml) cream
125g button mushrooms, sliced thinly
2 tablespoons finely grated parmesan cheese
¼ cup coarsely chopped fresh chives

1 Cut ciabatta into 1.5cm thick slices; halve any large slices crossways. Toast under hot grill until browned lightly; while still hot, rub one side of toast with three cloves of the garlic. Place toast in single layer on tray; drizzle half of the oil evenly over toast. *[Can be made 3 hours ahead to this stage and covered.]*

2 Crush remaining garlic. Heat remaining oil in medium non-stick frying pan; cook flat mushrooms, stirring over heat, until very soft. Add juice; stir over high heat until absorbed. Pour in cream; stir to combine. Gently stir in button mushrooms; stir over high heat until almost all liquid is absorbed. Remove from heat; stir in cheese.

3 Just before serving, top bruschetta with mushroom mixture; sprinkle with chives.

serves 8

per serving 22.7g fat; 1221kJ

olive, anchovy and caper bruschetta

PREPARATION TIME 15 MINUTES
COOKING TIME 5 MINUTES

½ loaf ciabatta (275g)
3 cloves garlic, halved
⅓ cup (80ml) olive oil
3 anchovy fillets, drained, chopped finely
½ cup (60g) seeded black olives, chopped finely
1 tablespoon drained baby capers
1 tablespoon lemon juice
⅓ cup (25g) parmesan cheese flakes
2 tablespoons marjoram

1 Cut ciabatta into 1.5cm thick slices; halve any large slices crossways. Toast under hot grill until browned lightly; while still hot, rub one side of toast with garlic. Place toast in single layer on tray; drizzle ¼ cup (60ml) of the oil evenly over toast. *[Can be made 3 hours ahead to this stage and covered.]*

2 Combine anchovy, olives, capers, juice and remaining oil in small bowl.

3 Just before serving, divide olive mixture among bruschetta; top with cheese then marjoram.

serves 8

per serving 11.3g fat; 792kJ

bruschetta with tomato and rocket

PREPARATION TIME 15 MINUTES
COOKING TIME 5 MINUTES

½ loaf ciabatta (275g)
3 cloves garlic, halved
¼ cup (60ml) olive oil
3 medium egg tomatoes (225g), chopped finely
½ small red onion (50g), chopped finely
25g baby rocket leaves

1 Cut ciabatta into 1.5cm thick slices; halve any large slices crossways. Toast under hot grill until browned lightly; while still hot, rub one side of toast with garlic. Place toast in single layer on tray; drizzle oil evenly over toast. *[Can be made 3 hours ahead to this stage and covered.]*

2 Combine tomato and onion in small bowl.

3 Just before serving, top bruschetta with tomato mixture, then rocket; sprinkle with freshly ground black pepper, if desired.

serves 8

per serving 7.8g fat; 628kJ

bruschetta

pizza

If you've only eaten the fast food variety, you haven't really tried pizza. Despite coming a long way from its cheese and tomato origins, the basic principle remains the same – fresh, yeasty bread dough topped with a range of tasty ingredients. Although purchased bases are convenient, our easy homemade ones will convert you!

marinara pizza

PREPARATION TIME 25 MINUTES ■ COOKING TIME 40 MINUTES

250g medium uncooked prawns

250g marinara seafood mix

1 tablespoon olive oil

1 medium white onion (150g), chopped finely

1 clove garlic, crushed

425g canned tomatoes

⅓ cup (80ml) dry white wine

30cm homemade or purchased pizza base

3 cloves garlic, crushed, extra

¼ cup (70g) tomato paste

2 teaspoons dried oregano

1 Peel and devein prawns. Rinse marinara mix under cold running water; drain well.

2 Heat oil in large frying pan; cook onion and garlic, stirring, until onion is soft. Add undrained crushed tomatoes and wine. Simmer, uncovered, until sauce thickens.

3 Add seafood; simmer, uncovered, 2 minutes or until seafood just changes colour. Remove seafood with slotted spoon. Continue simmering sauce until very thick.

4 Place pizza base on oiled pizza tray. Spread with combined garlic, paste and oregano. Spoon seafood, then sauce over pizza.

5 Bake, uncovered, in moderately hot oven about 20 minutes or until base is cooked though and seafood is tender.

serves 4

per serving 9.5g fat: 1601kJ

tip If you prefer to use just prawns for this pizza, you will need 750g medium uncooked prawns.

tomato
and onion pitta pizzas

PREPARATION TIME 15 MINUTES ■ COOKING TIME 15 MINUTES

4 wholemeal pitta

¼ cup (60ml) bottled tomato pasta sauce

1 cup (125g) grated cheddar cheese

2 medium tomatoes (380g), sliced thinly

1 medium brown onion (150g), sliced thinly

¼ cup (30g) seeded black olives, halved

1 Place pitta in single layer on lightly oiled oven tray. Spread each pitta with pasta sauce; top with half of the cheese. Top with tomato, onion and olives; sprinkle with remaining cheese.

2 Bake pizzas in hot oven about 15 minutes or until browned lightly.

serves 4

per serving 16.7g fat; 1633kJ

napoletana pizza

PREPARATION TIME 20 MINUTES (plus standing time) ■ COOKING TIME 30 MINUTES

300g mozzarella, sliced thinly

¼ cup coarsely torn basil

basic pizza dough

2 teaspoons (7g) instant yeast

½ teaspoon salt

2½ cups (375g) plain flour

1 cup (250ml) warm water

1 tablespoon olive oil

basic tomato pizza sauce

1 tablespoon olive oil

1 small white onion (80g), chopped finely

2 cloves garlic, crushed

425g canned tomatoes

¼ cup (70g) tomato paste

1 teaspoon sugar

1 tablespoon fresh oregano

1 Halve basic pizza dough; roll out each half on lightly floured surface to form 30cm round. Place on two oiled pizza trays. Spread each with half of the basic tomato pizza sauce; top with cheese.

2 Bake, uncovered, in moderately hot oven about 15 minutes or until crust is golden and cheese is bubbling. Sprinkle each with basil before serving.

basic pizza dough Combine yeast, salt and sifted flour in large bowl; mix well. Gradually stir in the water and oil. Knead on well floured surface about 10 minutes or until smooth and elastic. Place dough in large oiled bowl; stand in warm place about 30 minutes or until dough doubles in size. Knead dough on lightly floured surface until smooth. Roll out dough as required or to fit pizza tray.

basic tomato pizza sauce Heat oil in medium frying pan; cook onion, stirring occasionally, over low heat until soft and transparent. Stir in garlic, undrained, crushed tomatoes, paste, sugar and oregano. Simmer, uncovered, about 15 minutes or until mixture thickens. *[Can be made 2 days ahead and refrigerated, covered, or frozen for up to 6 months.]*

serves 6

per serving 18.1g fat; 1890kJ

store Basic pizza dough can be made 3 hours ahead and refrigerated, covered. Remove from refrigerator 10 minutes before using.

tip Purchased pizza bases can be used in place of the basic pizza dough.

roast garlic and potato pizza

PREPARATION TIME 25 MINUTES ■ COOKING TIME 1 HOUR 10 MINUTES

5 medium potatoes (1kg), halved

4 cloves garlic, crushed

¼ cup fresh oregano

1 large brown onion (200g), sliced thickly

¼ cup (60ml) olive oil

7 small tomatoes (910g), halved

2 teaspoons sugar

30cm round homemade or purchased pizza base

1½ cups (150g) coarsely grated mozzarella cheese

¼ cup finely shredded fresh basil

1 Boil, steam or microwave potato until just tender; drain. Cut each potato half in half again; place in large shallow baking dish with garlic, oregano and onion. Drizzle with 2 tablespoons of the oil. Bake, uncovered, in very hot oven about 20 minutes or until onion is soft and potato is browned lightly.

2 Meanwhile, combine tomato and remaining oil in medium baking dish; bake, uncovered, in very hot oven about 30 minutes or until tomato is browned and soft. Blend or process tomato with sugar until just chopped coarsely. *[Can be made a day ahead to this stage and refrigerated, covered.]*

3 Spread tomato mixture on pizza base; top with 1 cup of the cheese, then potato mixture. Sprinkle remaining cheese and basil over the top; bake, uncovered, in hot oven, uncovered, about 30 minutes or until cheese is browned and pizza base is crisp.

serves 4

per serving 25g fat; 2677kJ

vegetarian calzone

PREPARATION TIME 40 MINUTES (plus standing time) ■ COOKING TIME 50 MINUTES

2 teaspoons (7g) dry yeast

1 teaspoon sugar

1½ cups (375ml) warm water

4 cups (600g) plain flour

1 teaspoon salt

½ teaspoon cracked black pepper

2 tablespoons olive oil

**1 cup (125g) coarsely grated
cheddar cheese**

vegetable filling

**1 small eggplant (230g),
chopped coarsely**

coarse cooking salt

1 tablespoon olive oil

**1 large brown onion (200g),
chopped coarsely**

2 cloves garlic, crushed

**1 medium red capsicum (200g),
chopped coarsely**

**2 medium zucchini (240g),
chopped coarsely**

**2 trimmed sticks celery (150g),
chopped coarsely**

2 tablespoons tomato paste

½ cup (125ml) vegetable stock

1 Whisk yeast, sugar and the water together in small bowl. Cover; stand in warm place about 10 minutes or until mixture is frothy.

2 Place flour, salt and pepper in large bowl. Stir in yeast mixture and oil; mix to a firm dough. Turn dough onto floured surface; knead about 10 minutes or until smooth and elastic. Place dough in large oiled bowl. Cover; stand in warm place about 30 minutes or until doubled in size.

3 Transfer dough to floured surface; knead until smooth. Divide dough into four pieces; roll each piece to a 24cm round. Spread one half of each round with a quarter of the vegetable filling; top with a quarter of the cheese. Fold plain dough over cheese to enclose filling; press edges together.

4 Place calzone on oiled oven trays; brush with a little extra oil. Cut two small slits on top of each calzone; bake, uncovered, in hot oven about 20 minutes or until browned.

vegetable filling Place eggplant in strainer. Sprinkle with salt; stand 30 minutes. Rinse eggplant under cold running water; drain on absorbent paper. Heat oil in large frying pan; cook onion and garlic, stirring, until onion is soft. Add eggplant, capsicum, zucchini and celery; cook, stirring, about 5 minutes or until vegetables are soft. Add paste and stock. Cook, stirring, until mixture thickens; cool. *[Can be made a day ahead to this stage and refrigerated, covered, or frozen for up to 2 months.]*

serves 4

per serving 26.8g fat; 3497kJ

pepperoni in a flash

PREPARATION TIME 10 MINUTES ■ COOKING TIME 20 MINUTES

30cm homemade or purchased pizza base
1/3 cup (90g) tomato paste
2 teaspoons dried oregano
2 cups (200g) grated mozzarella cheese
1/4 cup (20g) grated parmesan cheese
150g sliced pepperoni
1/2 cup (80g) seeded black olives

1 Place pizza base on oiled pizza tray. Spread base with combined tomato paste and oregano; sprinkle with two-thirds of the combined cheeses. Top with pepperoni and olives, then remaining cheeses.

2 Bake, uncovered, in moderately hot oven about 20 minutes or until base is cooked through and cheese is bubbling.

serves 4

per serving 29g fat; 2311kJ

tip Any salami, cabanossi or ham can be substituted for the pepperoni.

pizza with prosciutto and ricotta

PREPARATION TIME 15 MINUTES ■ COOKING TIME 15 MINUTES

3 medium egg tomatoes (225g)

3 x 25cm homemade or purchased pizza bases

1/2 cup (140g) tomato paste

300g baby spinach

1 large red onion (300g), sliced thinly

9 slices prosciutto (135g), halved

1/4 cup loosely packed, coarsely chopped fresh basil

11/2 cups (300g) ricotta cheese

1/4 cup (40g) pine nuts

1/4 cup (60ml) olive oil

2 cloves garlic, crushed

1 Cut each tomato into eight wedges.

2 Place pizza bases on oven trays. Spread each base with a third of the tomato paste; top with equal amounts of tomato, spinach, onion, prosciutto, basil, cheese and pine nuts. Drizzle each pizza with equal amounts of combined oil and garlic.

3 Bake, uncovered, in very hot oven about 15 minutes or until pizza tops are browned lightly and bases are crisp.

serves 6

per serving 27.6g fat; 2934kJ

salami, mushroom and oregano pizza

PREPARATION TIME 15 MINUTES ■ COOKING TIME 20 MINUTES

30cm homemade or purchased pizza base

1/4 cup (70g) tomato paste

2 teaspoons dried oregano

1/3 cup (80ml) bottled tomato pasta sauce

1/2 cup (150g) coarsely chopped cooked silverbeet

50g button mushrooms, sliced thinly

100g sliced salami

3/4 cup (75g) grated mozzarella cheese

1 Place pizza base on lightly oiled pizza tray. Spread combined tomato paste and oregano over pizza base. Top with pasta sauce, silverbeet, mushrooms, then salami. Sprinkle with cheese.

2 Bake, uncovered, in moderately hot oven, about 20 minutes or until base is cooked through and cheese is bubbling.

serves 4

per serving   16.5g fat; 1596kJ

tips Split a purchased base in half for a thin crust pizza. Use cut-side up and bake about 5 minutes less than the time stated.

Use your choice of mild or hot salami for this pizza.

roasted tomato, goat cheese and chicken pizza

PREPARATION TIME 25 MINUTES ■ COOKING TIME 35 MINUTES

500g cherry tomatoes, halved
2 tablespoons balsamic vinegar
2 tablespoons brown sugar
2 chicken breast fillets (340g)
30cm round homemade or purchased pizza base
2 tablespoons coarsely chopped fresh coriander
80g goat cheese
40g rocket

1 Place tomatoes on oven tray lined with baking paper; drizzle with combined vinegar and sugar. Bake, uncovered, in very hot oven about 25 minutes or until tomatoes are soft.

2 Meanwhile, cook chicken on heated oiled grill plate (or grill or barbecue) until browned both sides and cooked through. Cool 5 minutes; cut into thin slices. Place pizza base on oven tray; bake, uncovered, in hot oven about 10 minutes or until browned lightly.

3 Top pizza with tomato, chicken, coriander and crumbled cheese. Bake, uncovered, in very hot oven, 10 minutes or until pizza is browned and crisp.

4 Just before serving, top with rocket.

serves 2

per serving 17.6g fat; 3278kJ

tips Lebanese bread can be substituted for prepared pizza base.
Use baking paper to prevent the skin of the tomatoes sticking to oven tray.

silverbeet and fetta pizza

PREPARATION TIME 25 MINUTES (plus standing time) ■ COOKING TIME 30 MINUTES

2 teaspoons (7g) dry yeast

1 teaspoon sugar

2¹/₂ cups (375g) plain flour

1 cup (250ml) warm water

¹/₂ teaspoon salt

2 tablespoons olive oil

¹/₄ cup (40g) semolina

500g silverbeet

1 cup (200g) crumbled fetta cheese

¹/₃ cup (25g) finely grated parmesan cheese

10 cherry tomatoes (100g), halved

tomato sauce

1 tablespoon olive oil

1 medium brown onion (150g), chopped coarsely

2 cloves garlic, crushed

425g canned tomatoes

¹/₂ cup (140g) tomato paste

¹/₄ cup coarsely chopped fresh basil

1 teaspoon sugar

1 Combine yeast, sugar, 1 tablespoon of the flour and the water in small bowl; whisk until yeast dissolves. Cover; stand in warm place about 10 minutes or until mixture is frothy.

2 Combine remaining sifted flour and salt in processor; pour in combined yeast mixture and oil while motor is operating. Process until dough forms a ball. Turn dough onto floured surface; knead 10 minutes or until dough is smooth and elastic. Place dough in oiled large bowl. Cover; stand in warm place about 30 minutes or until dough doubles in size.

3 Turn dough onto surface sprinkled with half of the semolina; knead 1 minute. Place dough on oiled large oven tray sprinkled with remaining semolina; press dough into a 32cm square.

4 Boil, steam or microwave silverbeet until wilted. Drain; cool. Squeeze as much liquid as possible from silverbeet; chop silverbeet finely. Spread pizza base with tomato sauce. Spread evenly with silverbeet, cheeses and tomato. Bake in very hot oven about 20 minutes.

tomato sauce Heat oil in medium saucepan; cook onion and garlic, stirring, until onion is soft. Stir in undrained crushed tomatoes, paste, basil and sugar; simmer, uncovered, about 5 minutes or until thickened.

serves 6

per serving 19.5g fat; 2022kJ

pesto, bocconcini
and artichoke pizza

PREPARATION TIME 10 MINUTES ■ COOKING TIME 25 MINUTES

**30cm homemade or purchased
  pizza base**

190g jar pesto

100g marinated eggplant slices

200g char-grilled capsicum slices

**2 drained marinated artichoke
  hearts, sliced thickly**

6 bocconcini (200g), sliced thickly

2 tablespoons pine nuts

1 Place pizza base on oiled pizza tray. Spread pesto over base; top with eggplant, capsicum and artichokes. Arrange bocconcini on top; sprinkle with pine nuts.

2 Bake, uncovered, in moderately hot oven about 20 minutes or until base is cooked through and cheese is bubbling.

serves 4

per serving 40.1g fat; 2581kJ

tip The same amount of ingredients used to top a 30cm pizza will top four mini pizza bases.

spinach, anchovy and olive pizza

30cm homemade or purchased pizza base
1/3 cup (80ml) bottled tomato pasta sauce
1/2 cup (150g) coarsely chopped cooked spinach
1/2 cup (50g) grated mozzarella cheese
1/3 cup (25g) grated parmesan cheese
1/4 cup (30g) grated cheddar cheese
1/2 cup (80g) black olives
6 anchovy fillets, drained

1 Place pizza base on lightly oiled pizza tray; spread with pasta sauce.

2 Squeeze as much liquid as possible from spinach. Spread spinach over pasta sauce; top with combined cheeses. Sprinkle olives and anchovies over top.

3 Bake, uncovered, in moderately hot oven about 20 minutes or until base is cooked through and cheese is bubbling.

serves 4

per serving 10.7g fat; 1347kJ

tip Use frozen spinach, which has been cooked and cooled, for this recipe.

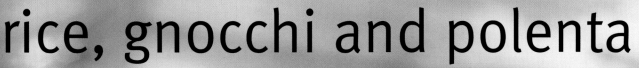

rice, gnocchi and polenta

While pasta might be popularly known as the national dish, there are also areas of Italy – principally in the rice- and corn-growing north – where rice, gnocchi and polenta enjoy a similar esteem. Here, creamy risotto, melt-in-the mouth gnocchi and golden polenta feature in a selection of delicious alternatives to pasta.

roasted pumpkin and rosemary risotto

PREPARATION TIME 20 MINUTES ■ COOKING TIME 40 MINUTES

1kg pumpkin, chopped coarsely

¼ cup (60ml) olive oil

1½ cups (300g) arborio rice

1 clove garlic, crushed

1 tablespoon fresh rosemary

1 litre (4 cups) hot vegetable stock

150g baby spinach

¼ cup (20g) coarsely grated parmesan cheese

¼ cup (60ml) cream

2 tablespoons parmesan cheese flakes

1 Combine pumpkin and half of the oil in baking dish. Bake, uncovered, in moderate oven, about 40 minutes or until pumpkin is tender.

2 Meanwhile, heat remaining oil in large saucepan. Add rice; stir to coat in oil. Add garlic and rosemary; cook, stirring, until fragrant.

3 Stir in 1 cup of the stock; cook, stirring, over low heat until liquid is absorbed.

4 Continue adding stock, in 1-cup batches, stirring after each addition. Total cooking time should be about 35 minutes or until rice is tender; remove from heat.

5 Stir in pumpkin, spinach, grated parmesan and cream. Stir over heat until hot. Serve topped with parmesan flakes.

serves 4

per serving 25.3g fat; 2484kJ

tip Leftover risotto can be made into patties and pan-fried. Serve topped with crisp prosciutto; dot with sour cream.

risotto cakes with basil sauce and pancetta

PREPARATION TIME 20 MINUTES ■ COOKING TIME 45 MINUTES

½ cup (125ml) dry white wine

1 medium brown onion (150g), chopped finely

1 clove garlic, crushed

1 cup (200g) arborio rice

3 cups (750ml) chicken stock

2 tablespoons finely chopped fresh parsley

2 tablespoons finely chopped fresh chives

2 tablespoons finely grated parmesan cheese

1 egg white, beaten lightly

4 slices pancetta (60g)

4 oak leaf lettuce leaves

basil sauce

1 teaspoon cornflour

1 teaspoon water

¾ cup (180ml) low-fat evaporated milk

1 tablespoon coarsely chopped fresh basil

1 Heat 2 tablespoons of the wine in large saucepan; cook onion and garlic, stirring, about 2 minutes or until onion softens.

2 Add rice and remaining wine; cook, stirring, about 3 minutes or until wine reduces by half. Stir in stock; bring to a boil. Reduce heat; simmer, covered, 15 minutes, stirring halfway through cooking. Remove from heat; stir in parsley, chives and cheese. Cool; stir in egg white. Using hands, shape risotto mixture into four patties. *[Can be made a day ahead to this stage and refrigerated, covered.]*

3 Place pancetta on oven tray. Bake, uncovered, in hot oven about 5 minutes or until crisp; drain on absorbent paper. Break pancetta into pieces.

4 Cook risotto cakes in large heated lightly oiled non-stick frying pan until browned both sides. Place cakes on oven tray; bake, uncovered, in moderate oven about 10 minutes or until hot.

5 Serve risotto cakes on lettuce leaves. Drizzle with basil sauce; top with pancetta.

basil sauce Blend cornflour with the water in small saucepan; add milk. Stir over heat until mixture boils and thickens slightly; stir in basil.

serves 4

per serving 3.6g fat; 1231kJ

pumpkin
gnocchi with rocket pesto

PREPARATION TIME 25 MINUTES ■ COOKING TIME 25 MINUTES

800g coarsely chopped pumpkin
1 tablespoon olive oil
2 large potatoes (600g), chopped coarsely
1 egg, beaten lightly
1 egg yolk
2 cups (300g) plain flour
2¹/₃ cups (580ml) cream

rocket pesto
1 cup firmly packed baby rocket
¹/₂ cup (90g) shelled pistachios, toasted
2 cloves garlic, quartered
¹/₂ cup (40g) coarsely grated parmesan cheese
¹/₄ cup (60ml) olive oil

1 Toss pumpkin with oil in large baking dish. Bake, uncovered, in hot oven about 45 minutes or until pumpkin is tender. Boil, steam or microwave potato until tender; drain.

2 Mash pumpkin and potato in large bowl until smooth; stir in egg and yolk. Using floured hand, mix in flour. Turn pumpkin mixture onto floured surface; knead about 2 minutes or until smooth.

3 Using floured hands, roll heaped teaspoons of pumpkin mixture into gnocchi-shaped ovals. Place each oval in palm of hand; press with inverted floured fork tines to flatten gnocchi slightly and make grooved imprint. *[Can be made a day ahead to this stage and refrigerated, covered, or frozen for up to 3 months.]*

4 Cook gnocchi, in batches, in large saucepan of boiling water; cook, uncovered, about 3 minutes or until gnocchi float to the surface. Remove from pan with slotted spoon; drain.

5 Working quickly, while gnocchi are cooking, heat cream with 2 tablespoons of the rocket pesto in medium saucepan. Serve gnocchi with cream sauce; top with additional rocket pesto to taste.

rocket pesto Blend or process rocket, nuts, garlic and cheese until chopped coarsely. With motor operating, gradually pour in oil; process until mixture forms a thick paste. *[Can be made a day ahead and refrigerated, covered, or frozen for up to 2 months.]*

serves 8

per serving 51.3g fat; 2943kJ
tip You will need about 1.25kg of unpeeled pumpkin for this recipe.

lemon risotto

PREPARATION TIME 15 MINUTES ■ COOKING TIME 40 MINUTES

1 litre (4 cups) chicken stock

1 cup (250ml) dry white wine

2 teaspoons finely grated lemon rind

1 tablespoon lemon juice

80g butter

1 medium brown onion (150g), chopped finely

2 cups (400g) arborio rice

3/4 cup (60g) finely grated parmesan cheese

2 tablespoons finely chopped fresh flat-leaf parsley

1 medium lemon (140g), quartered

1 Bring stock and wine to a boil in medium saucepan. Add rind and juice; reduce heat. Cover; keep hot.

2 Heat half of the butter in large saucepan; cook onion, stirring, until soft. Add rice; stir over medium heat until coated in butter mixture .

3 Stir 1 cup of the stock mixture into rice mixture; cook, stirring, over low heat until liquid is absorbed.

4 Continue adding stock mixture in 1-cup batches, stirring after each addition. Total cooking time should be about 35 minutes.

5 Remove pan from heat; serve topped with cheese and parsley. Accompany risotto with lemon quarters.

serves 4

per serving 22.1g fat; 2805kJ

risotto milanese

PREPARATION TIME 15 MINUTES ■ COOKING TIME 40 MINUTES

3¹/₂ cups (875ml) hot chicken stock

¹/₂ cup (125ml) dry white wine

¹/₄ teaspoon saffron

50g butter

1 large brown onion (200g), chopped finely

1³/₄ cups (350g) arborio rice

2 tablespoons grated parmesan cheese

1 Bring stock, wine and saffron to a boil in medium saucepan. Reduce heat; simmer, covered, while preparing onion and rice.

2 Heat half of the butter in large saucepan; cook onion, stirring until soft. Add rice; stir over medium heat until coated in butter mixture. Stir in 1 cup (250ml) of the stock mixture; cook, stirring, over low heat until liquid is absorbed.

3 Continue adding stock mixture in 1-cup batches, stirring after each addition until liquid is absorbed. Total cooking time should be about 35 minutes or until rice is tender.

4 Stir in remaining butter and cheese.

serves 2

per serving 25.5g fat; 3970kJ

gnocchi
with burnt butter and sage

PREPARATION TIME 25 MINUTES (plus refrigeration time) ■ COOKING TIME 25 MINUTES

3 large desiree potatoes (900g)
1 clove garlic, crushed
2 tablespoons milk
2 egg yolks
1/3 cup (25g) grated parmesan cheese
1 cup (150g) plain flour, approximately
125g butter, chopped coarsely
12 fresh sage leaves
1/4 cup (20g) parmesan cheese flakes, extra
freshly ground black pepper

1 Steam or boil whole unpeeled potatoes until tender; drain. Cool potatoes slightly; peel. Mash potatoes with a ricer, mouli or masher until smooth; stir in garlic and milk. Stir in egg yolks, grated parmesan and enough of the flour to form a firm dough.

2 Roll a quarter of the dough on lightly floured surface into a 2cm-thick sausage. Cut into 2cm lengths; roll into gnocchi-shaped ovals. Place each oval in palm of hand; press with inverted floured fork tines to flatten gnocchi slightly and make a grooved imprint. Place on lightly floured tray in single layer. Cover; refrigerate 1 hour. *[Can be made a day ahead to this stage and refrigerated, covered, or frozen for up to 3 months.]*

3 Cook gnocchi, in batches, in large saucepan of boiling water about 3 minutes or until gnocchi float to the surface. Remove from pan with slotted spoon; drain.

4 Meanwhile, cook butter in small shallow frying pan until just browned. Add sage; immediately remove from heat. Divide gnocchi among serving plates; drizzle with sage butter. Serve topped with parmesan flakes, and pepper.

serves 4

per serving 33.2g fat; 2483kJ
tips Pinkeye potatoes are also suitable for this recipe.
A ricer or mouli, available from kitchenware stores, will give the best result for smooth potato.

soft polenta with braised vegetables

PREPARATION TIME 15 MINUTES ■ COOKING TIME 15 MINUTES

Polenta is a cereal made from ground corn. Like an Italian version of mashed potatoes, it's an ideal companion for saucy dishes.

2½ cups (625ml) water

1 cup (170g) polenta

½ cup (40g) finely grated parmesan cheese

1 tablespoon olive oil

1 medium brown onion (150g), sliced thinly

1 clove garlic, crushed

200g button mushrooms, halved

2 medium green zucchini (240g), sliced thickly

8 medium yellow patty-pan squash (100g), quartered

600ml bottled tomato pasta sauce

¾ cup (180ml) vegetable stock

1 Bring the water to a boil in medium saucepan. Sprinkle polenta gradually into the water, stirring constantly. Cover, reduce heat to low; cook, stirring occasionally, about 10 minutes or until polenta thickens. Add cheese, stir until melted.

2 Meanwhile, heat oil in medium saucepan; cook onion and garlic, stirring, until onion softens. Add mushrooms; cook, stirring, 3 minutes. Add zucchini and squash; cook, stirring, 2 minutes. Add sauce and stock; bring to a boil. Reduce heat; simmer, covered, about 8 minutes or until vegetables are just tender.

3 Serve polenta with braised vegetables.

serves 4

per serving   10.5g fat; 1462kJ

tips   Braised vegetables can be prepared in advance and refrigerated, covered; reheat just before serving.

Serve with a tossed green salad and crusty Italian bread, such as ciabatta.

gnocchi al quattro formaggi

PREPARATION TIME 10 MINUTES ■ COOKING TIME 10 MINUTES

¼ cup (60ml) dry white wine

1 cup (250g) mascarpone cheese

1 cup (120g) coarsely grated
   fontina cheese

½ cup (40g) coarsely grated
   parmesan cheese

¼ cup (60ml) milk

625g gnocchi

75g gorgonzola cheese, crumbled

freshly ground black pepper

1 Bring wine to a boil in large saucepan. Boil, uncovered, until wine reduces by half; reduce heat. Add mascarpone; stir until mixture is smooth. Add fontina, parmesan and milk; cook, stirring, until cheeses melt and sauce is smooth.

2 Meanwhile, cook gnocchi, uncovered, in large saucepan of boiling water, until gnocchi rise to the surface. Remove with a slotted spoon; drain.

3 Add gnocchi and gorgonzola to sauce; toss gently to combine. Sprinkle with pepper.

serves 4

per serving 52.3g fat; 3068kJ

buttery wine
risotto with smoked salmon

PREPARATION TIME 10 MINUTES ■ COOKING TIME 40 MINUTES

1.5 litres (6 cups) chicken stock
1 cup (250ml) dry white wine
40g butter
1 medium leek (350g), chopped finely
2 cloves garlic, crushed
2 cups (400g) arborio rice
1/4 teaspoon ground turmeric
40g butter, chopped finely, extra
1/2 cup (40g) finely grated parmesan cheese
100g smoked salmon, chopped coarsely
2 teaspoons finely chopped fresh dill
50g baby spinach

1 Bring stock and wine to a boil in medium saucepan; reduce heat. Cover; keep hot.

2 Heat butter in large saucepan; cook leek and garlic, stirring, until leek is very soft. Add rice and turmeric; stir to coat in butter mixture. Stir in 1 cup of the stock mixture; cook, stirring, over low heat until liquid is absorbed.

3 Continue adding stock mixture in 1-cup batches, stirring after each addition. Total cooking time should be about 35 minutes or until rice is tender. Remove pan from heat; stir in extra butter, cheese, salmon, dill and spinach.

serves 4

per serving 23.1g fat; 2824kJ

spinach gnocchi

PREPARATION TIME 30 MINUTES ■ COOKING TIME 20 MINUTES

500g spinach

1¼ cups (250g) ricotta cheese

1 cup (80g) finely grated parmesan cheese

1 egg, beaten lightly

¼ teaspoon ground nutmeg

plain flour

45g butter, melted

1 Steam or microwave spinach until wilted. Rinse under cold running water; drain well. Squeeze as much liquid as possible from spinach; chop finely.

2 Combine spinach, ricotta, half of the parmesan, egg and nutmeg in medium bowl.

3 Using tablespoon and palm of hand, roll mixture into egg shapes.

4 Roll gnocchi lightly in flour. Cook gnocchi, in batches, in large saucepan of boiling water, uncovered, about 3 minutes or until gnocchi float to the surface. Remove from pan with slotted spoon; drain.

5 Arrange gnocchi in ovenproof dish. Pour butter over gnocchi; sprinkle with remaining parmesan. *[Can be made a day ahead to this stage and refrigerated, covered; reheat in moderate oven about 20 minutes or until hot.]* Cook under moderately hot grill until cheese turns golden brown.

serves 4

per serving 25.1g fat; 1376kJ

gnocchi alla romana

PREPARATION TIME 30 MINUTES (plus refrigerating time) ■ COOKING TIME 40 MINUTES

3 cups (750ml) milk

1½ teaspoons salt

pinch ground nutmeg

⅔ cup (110g) semolina

1 egg, beaten lightly

1½ cups (120g) grated parmesan cheese

60g butter, melted

1 Bring milk, salt and nutmeg to a boil in medium saucepan; reduce heat. Gradually add semolina, stirring constantly with wooden spoon.

2 Continue cooking, uncovered, stirring often, about 10 minutes, or until spoon can stand upright in centre. Remove from heat.

3 Combine egg and 1 cup (80g) of the cheese in small bowl. Add to semolina mixture; stir well. Spread mixture onto well-oiled 26cm x 32cm swiss roll pan; using wet spatula smooth until 5mm thick. Refrigerate about 1 hour or until semolina is firm.

4 Cut semolina into circles using 4cm pastry cutter. Arrange circles, overlapping, in greased shallow ovenproof dish. Pour over butter; sprinkle with remaining cheese. Bake in moderate oven about 15 minutes or until crisp and golden.

serves 4

per serving 31.4g fat; 2009kJ

polenta

PREPARATION TIME 15 MINUTES (plus standing time) ■ COOKING TIME 50 MINUTES

This is a specialty of northern Italy, particularly popular around Venice. Served plain, it is often accompanied by bolognese sauce; or it can be fried and served as an accompaniment to any meat. Hot, fried polenta can also be topped with anchovies and sliced olives or other toppings and served as crostini.

2 litres (8 cups) water
2 teaspoons salt
2 cups (340g) polenta
¼ cup (60ml) olive oil

1 Combine the water and salt in large saucepan; bring to a boil. Gradually sprinkle polenta over the water, stirring constantly with wooden spoon; make sure polenta has no lumps.

2 Reduce heat to low, as mixture may bubble and spatter; partially covering the saucepan is a good idea. Continue cooking, stirring, about 30 minutes or until polenta is very thick and spoon can stand upright in centre. *[Polenta can be served at this point, piled onto a plate.]*

3 Spoon mixture into greased 20cm x 30cm lamington pan; spread mixture out evenly. Allow to become cold; leave at room temperature a few hours.

4 Turn polenta out of pan; cut into 4cm slices. Heat oil in large frying pan until very hot; reduce heat. Gently fry polenta slices until golden brown both sides.

serves 4

per serving 15.4g fat; 1678kJ

tomato, bocconcini and basil salad

PREPARATION TIME 10 MINUTES

4 medium tomatoes (520g)
500g large bocconcini cheese
¼ cup coarsely chopped fresh basil

dressing
¼ cup (60ml) extra virgin olive oil
2 teaspoons balsamic vinegar
1 clove garlic, crushed
1 teaspoon caster sugar

1 Cut tomatoes and cheese into 5mm-thick slices.

2 Layer tomatoes and cheese alternately on serving plate; sprinkle with basil and dressing.

dressing Combine ingredients in screw-top jar; shake well.

serves 6

per serving 21.9g fat; 1114kJ
store Salad can be made 3 hours ahead and refrigerated, covered.
tip Mozzarella can be substituted for the bocconcini; stand 30 minutes before serving.

eggplant and mozzarella slices

PREPARATION TIME 15 MINUTES
COOKING TIME 15 MINUTES

2 medium eggplant (600g), peeled
250g mozzarella cheese
8 large basil leaves
¼ cup (60ml) olive oil

1 Cut eggplant into 2cm-thick rounds (you will need eight rounds). Split each round in half, horizontally, taking care not to cut all the way through. Gently open out rounds.

2 Cut cheese into eight slices. Place cheese in each of the eggplant rounds. Place one basil leaf on each piece of cheese. Fold over eggplant; trim cheese to size of eggplant if necessary. *[Can be made 3 hours ahead to this stage and refrigerated, covered.]*

3 Heat oil in medium non-stick frying pan. Cook eggplant over medium heat until browned both sides and tender and cheese begins to melt.

serves 8

per serving 13.9g fat; 701kJ
tip Thin slices of pancetta can be placed under the cheese.

pears and parmesan

PREPARATION TIME 5 MINUTES
COOKING TIME 5 MINUTES

½ loaf ciabatta (275g), sliced thinly
2 tablespoons olive oil
6 medium corella pears (665g)
180g parmesan cheese

1 Brush both sides of ciabatta slices with oil. Cook,
   in batches, on heated oiled grill plate (or grill
   or barbecue).

2 Place washed and unpeeled pears on serving
   plates. Divide cheese among plates; serve with
   ciabatta toast.

serves 6

per serving 17.1g fat; 1486kJ
tip Beurre bosc pears can be substituted for corella pears.
Halve or quarter pears; brush cut edges with lemon juice to
stop them browning.

figs with prosciutto

PREPARATION TIME 10 MINUTES

4 medium ripe figs (240g)
8 slices prosciutto (120g)
50g baby rocket
2 tablespoons extra virgin olive oil

1 Gently break open figs. Arrange figs and
   prosciutto on four serving plates.

2 Toss rocket with oil; divide among plates. Sprinkle
   with sea salt flakes and freshly ground black
   pepper, if desired.

serves 4

per serving 11.1g fat; 610kJ
tip Prosciutto is also great served with fresh rockmelon.
For a finger food treat, try wrapping cubes of melon in
prosciutto, twist the ends like bonbons and serve.

italian classics

seafood

Italy's extensive coastline and highly developed fishing industry mean that seafood dishes are enjoyed all over the country. Soups, stews and sauces are rich with abundant shellfish of all kinds, lightly fried mixed seafood is a specialty of several regions, and freshly-caught fish is grilled and pan-fried with an almost endless variety of different herbs and flavourings depending upon regional preference.

slow simmered octopus

PREPARATION TIME 20 MINUTES ■ COOKING TIME 1 HOUR 45 MINUTES

1kg baby octopus

1 tablespoon olive oil

**1 large brown onion (200g),
chopped coarsely**

3 cloves garlic, crushed

1 cup (250ml) dry red wine

850g canned tomatoes

**6 canned anchovy fillets,
chopped coarsely**

¼ cup (70g) tomato paste

**¼ cup coarsely chopped
fresh oregano**

1 Cut heads from octopus just below eyes. Discard heads; remove beaks. Wash octopus; quarter each octopus.

2 Heat oil in large saucepan; cook onion and garlic, stirring, until onion is soft.

3 Add octopus; cook, stirring, until just changed in colour.

4 Add wine; cook, stirring, about 5 minutes or until liquid reduces by about a third.

5 Add undrained crushed tomatoes and remaining ingredients; simmer, uncovered, about 1½ hours or until octopus is tender.

serves 4

per serving 8.1g fat; 1370kJ

store Recipe best made a day ahead, to allow the flavours to develop; can be refrigerated, covered, up to 2 days.

steamed garlic and herb mussels

PREPARATION TIME 30 MINUTES ■ COOKING TIME 25 MINUTES

**80 medium black mussels
(approximately 2kg)**

2 tablespoons olive oil

8 cloves garlic, crushed

**4 fresh red thai chillies, seeded,
chopped finely**

**1 tablespoon finely grated
lemon rind**

1 cup (250ml) lemon juice

1 cup (250ml) dry white wine

**1/2 cup finely chopped fresh
flat-leaf parsley**

1/3 cup finely chopped fresh basil

1 Scrub mussels; remove beards.

2 Heat oil in large saucepan; cook garlic, chilli and rind, stirring, about 2 minutes
or until fragrant. Add mussels, juice and wine; bring to a boil. Cook, covered,
about 5 minutes or until mussels open (discard any that do not open). Remove
mussels from pan.

3 Bring pan liquid to a boil; cook, uncovered, about 10 minutes or until mixture
thickens slightly. Stir in parsley and basil.

4 Return mussels to pan; simmer, stirring, until heated through.

serves 6

per serving 5.9g fat; 514kJ

squid and crisp prosciutto

PREPARATION TIME 15 MINUTES ■ COOKING TIME 15 MINUTES

1kg squid hoods
2 egg whites
1 teaspoon sea salt
1 teaspoon cracked black pepper
vegetable oil, for deep-frying

crisp prosciutto

120g thinly sliced prosciutto
2 tablespoons brown sugar
1 tablespoon warm water

garlic sauce

2 egg yolks
2 teaspoons lemon juice
2 cloves garlic, crushed
3/4 cup (180ml) olive oil

1 Cut squid in half lengthways. Score inside of each piece; cut into 2cm-wide strips.

2 Whisk egg whites, salt and pepper in small bowl.

3 Heat oil in large frying pan. Dip squid in egg mixture. Deep-fry, in batches, until squid is tender; drain on absorbent paper.

4 Serve squid with crisp prosciutto and garlic sauce.

crisp prosciutto Dip each prosciutto slice in combined sugar and water. Fold in half lengthways; twist into rosette shape. Place on oiled oven tray; bake, uncovered, in hot oven about 10 minutes or until browned and crisp.

garlic sauce Blend or process yolks, juice and garlic until smooth. With motor operating, gradually add oil in thin stream; process until sauce thickens. Transfer to small bowl; refrigerate, covered, until required.

serves 4

per serving 62.4g fat; 3280kJ
tips Cuttlefish can be substituted for the squid hoods.
If sauce is too thick, stir in a teaspoon or two of warm water to thin.

garfish with leek, prosciutto and prawns

PREPARATION TIME 35 MINUTES ■ COOKING TIME 15 MINUTES

1 medium leek (350g)
12 large cooked prawns (250g)
12 garfish (820g), butterflied
12 slices prosciutto (190g)
1 cup (280g) roasted vegetable pesto
2 medium yellow zucchini (240g)
2 medium green zucchini (240g)

1 Cut leek in half lengthways. Cut into 10cm lengths; separate layers. Drop leek into medium saucepan of boiling water; drain. Rinse under cold water; drain.

2 Shell and devein prawns.

3 Flatten garfish with rolling pin. Place fish skin-side down on board; line with pieces of leek, then a slice of prosciutto. Spread each with 1 teaspoon of the pesto; top with a prawn. Starting from head of fish, roll to enclose prawn; secure with toothpick. *[Can be made a day ahead to this stage and refrigerated, covered.]*

4 Cut zucchini lengthways into 5mm-thick slices. Cook on heated oiled grill plate (or grill or barbecue) until browned and tender. Cover; keep warm.

5 Cook fish on grill plate until cooked through. Serve fish with char-grilled zucchini.

serves 4

per serving 10g fat; 1246kJ

tip Roasted vegetable pesto is available from most supermarkets; alternatively, you can use your favourite flavoured pesto.

clams with tomato dressing

PREPARATION TIME 30 MINUTES ■ COOKING TIME 10 MINUTES

2.5kg clams, scrubbed

½ cup (125ml) dry white wine

**1 small red onion (100g),
chopped finely**

2 cloves garlic, crushed

2 tablespoons lemon juice

2 tablespoons white wine vinegar

½ cup (125ml) olive oil

**5 large tomatoes (1.25kg),
chopped coarsely**

4 green onions, sliced thinly

**2 tablespoons coarsely chopped
fresh coriander**

1 Rinse clams under cold running water; drain. Place clams in large saucepan with wine. Cover; bring to a boil. Reduce heat; simmer about 5 minutes or until shells open (discard any clams that do not open).

2 Meanwhile, heat large oiled saucepan; cook red onion and garlic over medium heat until browned lightly. Add combined juice, vinegar and oil; cook, stirring, about 2 minutes or until thickened slightly.

3 Drain clams; discard liquid.

4 Gently toss clams with tomato, green onion, coriander and red onion mixture.

serves 4

per serving 30.7g fat; 1584kJ

blue-eye
with caper and herb crust

PREPARATION TIME 20 MINUTES ■ COOKING TIME 20 MINUTES

1 cup (155g) pine nuts
¼ cup (40g) rolled oats
¼ cup (35g) white sesame seeds
2 cups (200g) packaged breadcrumbs
½ teaspoon dry mustard
1 tablespoon grated lemon rind
1 tablespoon lemon juice
1 egg, beaten lightly
1 tablespoon honey
2 tablespoons chopped fresh parsley
2 tablespoons chopped fresh lemon thyme
2 tablespoons drained capers, chopped coarsely
1 cup (80g) grated parmesan cheese
8 blue-eye cutlets (1.5kg)
plain flour
2 eggs, beaten lightly, extra
½ cup (125ml) vegetable oil

1 Process pine nuts, oats and seeds until chopped finely; transfer to large bowl. Stir in breadcrumbs, mustard, rind, juice, egg, honey, herbs, capers and cheese; mix well. Toss fish in flour; shake away excess. Dip fish in extra egg, then in breadcrumb mixture. *[Can be made 3 hours ahead to this stage and refrigerated, covered.]*

2 Heat oil in large frying pan; cook fish, in batches, until browned lightly both sides. Transfer to large oven tray; bake, uncovered, in moderate oven about 15 minutes or until cutlets are tender. Serve with lemon wedges and asparagus spears, if desired.

serves 8

per serving 40.3g fat; 2687kJ

walnut gremolata fish

PREPARATION TIME 25 MINUTES ■ COOKING TIME 30 MINUTES

⅓ cup (35g) walnut pieces, toasted, chopped finely

2 tablespoons finely chopped lemon rind

¼ cup finely chopped fresh parsley

2 cloves garlic, crushed

4 medium potatoes (800g), quartered

40g butter, chopped coarsely

¼ cup (60ml) milk

4 firm white fish fillets (640g)

1 tablespoon olive oil

1 Combine nuts, rind, parsley and half of the garlic in small bowl; cover gremolata.

2 Boil, steam or microwave potato until tender; drain. Mash potato with butter, milk and remaining garlic; keep warm.

3 Meanwhile, brush fish with oil; cook, skin-side down first, on heated oiled grill plate (or grill or barbecue) until browned both sides and cooked through.

4 Serve fish with garlic mash; top with gremolata.

serves 4

per serving 24.9g fat; 1964kJ

tip We used bream fillets for this recipe, but any firm white fish fillets are suitable.

char-grilled seafood salad
with gremolata dressing

PREPARATION TIME 30 MINUTES (plus marinating time) ■ COOKING TIME 20 MINUTES

24 large uncooked prawns (1kg)

500g squid hoods

500g cleaned baby octopus

1 tablespoon olive oil

1 tablespoon finely chopped lemon rind

1 clove garlic, chopped finely

1 medium green cucumber (170g)

100g mixed sprouts

gremolata dressing

1/4 cup (60ml) olive oil

1 tablespoon finely chopped lemon rind

1 clove garlic, chopped finely

2 tablespoons lemon juice

2 tablespoons coarsely chopped fresh flat-leaf parsley

1 Shell and devein prawns, leaving heads and tails intact. Cut squid in half lengthways; score inside surface of each piece. Cut squid into 5cm-wide strips. Remove and discard heads from octopus.

2 Combine seafood in large bowl with oil, rind and garlic; refrigerate, covered, until required. *[Can be made a day ahead to this stage.]*

3 Cook seafood, in batches, on heated oiled grill plate (or grill or barbecue) until prawns just change colour, and squid and octopus are tender.

4 Using vegetable peeler, slice cucumber into ribbons. Combine cucumber with sprouts in medium bowl.

5 Serve seafood on cucumber mixture; drizzle with gremolata dressing.

gremolata dressing Combine ingredients in screw-top jar; shake well.

serves 6

per serving 14.7g fat; 1238kJ

fish milanese

PREPARATION TIME 20 MINUTES (plus marinating time) ■ COOKING TIME 10 MINUTES

1 small brown onion (80g), chopped finely
2 tablespoons lemon juice
⅓ cup (80ml) olive oil
4 fish fillets
plain flour
2 eggs, beaten lightly
1 tablespoon milk
1 cup (100g) packaged breadcrumbs
1 tablespoon olive oil, extra
120g butter
1 clove garlic, crushed
2 teaspoons finely chopped fresh parsley

1 Combine onion, juice and oil in medium shallow bowl; mix well. Add fish; spoon mixture over fish to coat thoroughly. Cover; refrigerate 1 hour, turning occasionally.

2 Remove fish from marinade. Coat lightly with flour; shake away excess. Combine egg and milk in small bowl; dip fish into egg mixture. Coat in breadcrumbs; press on firmly. *[Can be made 3 hours ahead to this stage and refrigerated, covered.]*

3 Heat extra oil and half of the butter in large frying pan. Cook fish about 3 minutes each side, or until cooked through; drain on absorbent paper.

4 Heat remaining butter in small saucepan. Cook garlic until butter turns light golden brown; add parsley. Pour browned butter over fish.

serves 4

per serving 52.4g fat; 2602kJ

calamari

PREPARATION TIME 15 MINUTES ■ COOKING TIME 15 MINUTES

1 egg
2 tablespoons milk
1kg calamari rings, sliced thinly
2 cups (200g) packaged breadcrumbs
vegetable oil for deep-frying

1 Beat egg and milk in small bowl. Dip calamari in egg mixture; drain away excess. Toss in breadcrumbs; press breadcrumbs on firmly. *[Can be made 3 hours ahead to this stage and refrigerated, covered.]*

2 Heat oil in large saucepan. Deep-fry calamari, in batches, about 2 minutes or until golden brown; drain on absorbent paper. Serve with lemon wedges and tartare sauce, if desired.

serves 4

per serving 19.2g fat; 1474kJ

tips Two cloves of crushed garlic can be added to the egg mixture.
Calamari can be shallow-fried. Heat a small amount of oil in large frying pan; the oil should reach only halfway up the side of each calamari ring. Cook calamari rings in hot oil, about 2 minutes each side, or until golden brown.

fritto misto

PREPARATION TIME 35 MINUTES ■ COOKING TIME 20 MINUTES

500g uncooked king prawns
500g small squid
250g white fish fillets
vegetable oil for deep-frying
250g scallops

batter

1 cup (150g) self-raising flour
¼ teaspoon bicarbonate of soda
pinch salt
1 cup (250ml) water, approximately

1 Shell and devein prawns, leaving tails intact. Clean squid; cut into thin rings. Cut fish into 5cm pieces.

2 Heat oil in large saucepan. Dip prawns, squid, fish and scallops into batter; drain off excess. Deep-fry seafood in hot oil, in batches, until golden brown. Drain on absorbent paper. Serve hot with tartare sauce, if desired.

batter Combine flour, soda and salt in small bowl. Gradually add the water, stirring until batter is smooth. If batter is too thick, add a little more water.

serves 6

per serving 17.6g fat; 1127kJ

garlic marinated prawns

PREPARATION TIME 30 MINUTES (plus refrigeration time) ■ COOKING TIME 10 MINUTES

1 kg uncooked king prawns
3/4 cup (50g) stale breadcrumbs
6 cloves garlic, crushed
1/2 cup (125ml) olive oil
freshly ground black pepper
1/4 cup (60ml) lemon juice

1 Remove heads from prawns. Using sharp scissors, cut though shells from head to tail, leaving shells intact. Remove vein from prawns.

2 Combine breadcrumbs, garlic, oil and enough of the pepper to season, in large bowl. Add prawns; rub in breadcrumb mixture, trying to get breadcrumbs under shells if possible. Cover; refrigerate 1 hour. *[Can be made a day ahead to this stage.]*

3 Cook prawns, in batches, on heated oiled grill plate (or grill or barbecue), until just cooked through. Sprinkle with juice just before serving.

serves 4

per serving 39.8g fat; 1743kJ

sardines with tomatoes and caper dressing

PREPARATION TIME 20 MINUTES ■ COOKING TIME 10 MINUTES

16 fresh sardines (750g), cleaned

4 medium egg tomatoes (300g), sliced thickly

1 small red onion (100g), sliced thinly

1 tablespoon coarsely chopped fresh flat-leaf parsley

caper dressing

⅓ cup (80ml) red wine vinegar

¼ cup (60ml) extra virgin olive oil

1 tablespoon drained baby capers

1 clove garlic, crushed

1 tablespoon finely chopped fresh parsley

1 To butterfly the sardines, cut through the underside of the fish to the tail. Break backbone at tail; peel away backbone. Trim sardines.

2 Cook sardines on heated, oiled grill plate (or grill or barbecue), in batches, until browned both sides and just cooked through. Serve with tomato and onion. Spoon over caper dressing; top with parsley.

caper dressing Combine ingredients in screw-top jar; shake well.

serves 4

per serving 33.9g fat; 2039kJ

tip Have sardines cleaned and the heads removed at the fish monger; they may even butterfly them for you.

fish with chilli sherry vinegar

PREPARATION TIME 5 MINUTES ■ COOKING TIME 8 MINUTES

1 tablespoon garlic olive oil

4 blue-eye fillets, skin on (800g)

chilli sherry vinegar

¼ cup (60ml) garlic olive oil

1½ tablespoons sherry vinegar

1 teaspoon dried chilli flakes

2 tablespoons coarsely chopped fresh flat-leaf parsley

1 Heat oil in large non-stick frying pan; cook fish, flesh side down, until well browned. Turn fish; cook until browned and just cooked through.

2 Spoon chilli sherry vinegar over fish. Serve with lemon wedges and steamed zucchini and beans, if desired.

chilli sherry vinegar Place oil, vinegar, chilli and parsley in clean small saucepan; stir over low heat until just warm – do not overheat.

serves 4

per serving 19.7g fat; 1332kJ

tip Red or white wine vinegar can be substituted for the sherry vinegar.

cioppino

PREPARATION TIME 30 MINUTES ■ COOKING TIME 45 MINUTES

2 uncooked blue swimmer crabs (700g)

16 large uncooked prawns (500g)

450g swordfish steaks

1 tablespoon olive oil

1 medium brown onion (150g), chopped coarsely

2 trimmed sticks celery (150g), chopped coarsely

3 cloves garlic, crushed

6 medium tomatoes (1kg), chopped coarsely

415g canned tomato puree

½ cup (125ml) dry white wine

1⅓ cups (330ml) fish stock

1 teaspoon sugar

200g clams, scrubbed

200g scallops

2 tablespoons finely shredded fresh basil

⅓ cup coarsely chopped fresh flat-leaf parsley

1 Slip sharp knife under top of crab shell at back; lever off shell. Remove and discard whitish gills. Rinse well under cold running water. Using cleaver, chop each crab into pieces. Shell and devein prawns, leaving tails intact. Chop fish into 2cm pieces.

2 Heat oil in large saucepan; cook onion, celery and garlic, stirring, until onion is soft. Add tomato; cook, stirring, 5 minutes or until pulpy. Stir in puree, wine, stock and sugar; simmer, covered, 20 minutes.

3 Add crab and clams to pan; simmer, covered, 10 minutes (discard any clams that do not open). Add prawns, fish and scallops; cook, stirring occasionally, about 5 minutes, or until seafood changes colour and is cooked through. Stir in herbs.

serves 6

per serving 7.1g fat; 1068kJ

tips Substitute any firm-fleshed fish for the swordfish.

Originating in San Francisco's large Italian fishing community, cioppino is an Italian-American fish stew.

pan-fried fish steaks
with rosemary and oregano

PREPARATION TIME 5 MINUTES ■ COOKING TIME 7 MINUTES

4 firm white fish steaks (800g)

¼ cup (60ml) lemon juice

½ cup (125ml) extra virgin olive oil

1 teaspoon salt

2 teaspoons finely chopped fresh oregano

2 teaspoons finely chopped fresh rosemary

1 Cook fish on heated oiled grill plate (or grill or barbecue) until cooked through; turn once during cooking.

2 Meanwhile, combine remaining ingredients in screw-top jar; shake well.

3 Brush both sides of hot fish with herb dressing; serve with any remaining dressing and patty-pan squash, if desired.

serves 4

per serving 32.9g fat; 1924kJ

tip We used blue-eye cod cutlets for this recipe, but any firm white fish cutlets are suitable.

sardines with parmesan crumbs
and fresh tomato sauce

PREPARATION TIME 12 MINUTES (plus refrigeration time) ■ COOKING TIME 30 MINUTES

16 sardine fillets (250g)

1/4 cup (35g) plain flour

2 tablespoons milk

1 egg

2 cups (140g) stale breadcrumbs

**11/2 cups (120g) coarsely grated
parmesan cheese**

vegetable oil, for shallow-frying

fresh tomato sauce

1 tablespoon olive oil

**1 large brown onion (200g),
sliced thinly**

2 cloves garlic, crushed

**5 medium tomatoes (1kg),
chopped coarsely**

2 teaspoons sugar

1/3 cup (80ml) dry white wine

**2 tablespoons coarsely chopped
fresh basil**

1 Coat fish in flour; shake away excess. Dip fish in combined milk and egg; coat in combined breadcrumbs and cheese. Cover; refrigerate 30 minutes.

2 Heat oil in large frying pan. Shallow-fry fish, in batches, until browned and just cooked through; drain on absorbent paper. Serve fish with fresh tomato sauce; garnish with extra basil, if desired.

fresh tomato sauce Heat oil in medium saucepan; cook onion and garlic, stirring, until onion is soft. Add tomato, sugar and wine; simmer, uncovered, about 20 minutes or until sauce thickens. Stir in basil. *[Can be made 2 days ahead and refrigerated, covered, or frozen for up to 6 months.]*

serves 4

per serving 38.2g fat; 2788kJ

scampi with risotto triangles

PREPARATION TIME 30 MINUTES (plus refrigeration time) ■ COOKING TIME 50 MINUTES

24 uncooked scampi (1.2kg)

½ cup (125ml) olive oil

3 teaspoons finely grated lemon rind

⅓ cup (80ml) lemon juice

½ teaspoon cracked black pepper

2 tablespoons chopped fresh dill

100g rocket, trimmed

risotto triangles

¼ cup (60ml) olive oil

1 medium brown onion (150g), chopped finely

1 cup (200g) arborio rice

½ cup (125ml) dry white wine

3 cups (750ml) hot vegetable stock

½ cup (40g) finely grated parmesan cheese

plain flour

1 Prepare scampi; discard heads, leaving meat in shell.

2 Combine oil, rind, juice, pepper and dill in jug. Place scampi in large bowl; pour over a third of the marinade.

3 Cook scampi in heated large saucepan, stirring, about 3 minutes or until cooked through. Serve scampi, on rocket, with risotto triangles; drizzle with reserved marinade.

risotto triangles Coat 23cm-square slab cake pan with cooking-oil spray; line base and two sides with baking paper, extending paper 2cm above edge of pan. Heat 1 tablespoon of the oil in medium saucepan; cook onion, stirring, until soft. Add rice; stir to coat with oil. Add wine; cook, stirring, until wine is absorbed. Stir in stock; cook, uncovered, stirring occasionally, about 20 minutes or until rice is just tender and liquid is absorbed. Stir in cheese; press risotto into prepared pan. Cover; refrigerate 3 hours or overnight. Cut risotto into four squares; cut each square into four triangles. Coat triangles in flour; shake off excess. Heat remaining oil in large saucepan; cook risotto triangles, in batches, until browned both sides and heated through. Drain on absorbent paper.

serves 4

per serving 51g fat; 3658kJ

meat

While Italy both produces and enjoys excellent beef, lamb and pork, it is nonetheless

veal dishes for which the country is justifiably most famous. They're well represented

here – melt-in-the-mouth scallopini and Milan's famous osso buco, to name but two.

But veal is only part of the story, and all kinds of meat dishes feature

in the delicious and authentic recipes on the following pages.

vitello tonnato

PREPARATION TIME 40 MINUTES ■ COOKING TIME 1 HOUR 30 MINUTES (plus cooling time)

1.5kg nut of veal

**45g canned flat anchovy
  fillets, drained**

1 clove garlic, sliced thinly

**2 medium carrots (240g),
  chopped finely**

**3 trimmed sticks celery (225g),
  chopped finely**

**2 medium brown onions
  (300g), quartered**

6 sprigs parsley

1.25 litres (5 cups) chicken stock

1½ cups (375ml) dry white wine

1½ tablespoons capers

tuna sauce

¾ cup (180ml) vegetable oil

1 egg yolk

100g canned tuna, drained

2 tablespoons lemon juice

¼ cup (60ml) cream

1 Using tip of sharp knife, make shallow cuts along length of veal. Cut four anchovy fillets into 1cm lengths; reserve remaining anchovies. Insert anchovy pieces and garlic into each cut in veal. Place veal in large saucepan; cover with cold water. Bring to a boil; boil 1 minute, uncovered. Drain veal; rinse under cold running water.

2 Return veal to pan with carrot, celery, onion, parsley, stock and wine; bring to a boil. Reduce heat; simmer, partly covered, about 1½ hours or until veal is tender. Remove veal from stock; leave to cool. Reserve ¼ cup stock for sauce; cool. *[Can be made a day ahead to this stage and refrigerated, covered.]*

3 Cut veal into thin slices. Dip veal into sauce and arrange in overlapping slices around plate. Serve remainder of sauce separately; sprinkle with capers.

tuna sauce Cover reserved anchovy fillets with water; stand 10 minutes. Drain; pat dry with absorbent paper. Place oil, egg yolk, tuna, anchovy and juice in blender; blend until smooth. Place mixture in small bowl; stir in cream and reserved stock. *[Can be made a day ahead and refrigerated, covered.]*

serves 6

per serving 39.4g fat; 2785kJ

veal scallopini

PREPARATION TIME 10 MINUTES ■ COOKING TIME 20 MINUTES

4 veal steaks (320g)

30g butter

1 small brown onion (80g), chopped finely

¼ cup (60ml) dry sherry

2 teaspoons plain flour

½ cup (125ml) beef stock

125g button mushrooms, sliced thinly

2 tablespoons cream

1 Remove fat from veal; pound veal out thinly.

2 Melt butter in large frying pan; cook veal, while butter is foaming, about 3 minutes, turning once. Remove from pan; cook onion until soft. Pour in sherry.

3 Bring sherry to a boil. Stir in blended flour and stock; stir until sauce comes to a boil.

4 Return veal to pan. Add mushrooms; mix well. Cover pan; simmer gently 10 minutes. Stir in cream; stir until heated through.

serves 4

per serving 13.8g fat; 1206kJ

braised pork with fresh sage

PREPARATION TIME 15 MINUTES ■ COOKING TIME 1 HOUR 30 MINUTES

90g butter
1.5kg rack of pork (6 cutlets)
2 medium carrots (240g), sliced thickly
6 baby onions (150g), peeled
4 cloves garlic, peeled
2 bay leaves
6 sprigs fresh thyme
1¹/₃ cups (330ml) dry white wine

fresh sage sauce

15g butter
1 tablespoon plain flour
1 tablespoon fresh sage

1 Melt butter in large flameproof dish; cook pork until browned each side. Remove pork from dish. Place carrot, onion, garlic, bay leaves and thyme in dish; stir over heat about 5 minutes or until just browned. Return pork to dish with wine; transfer to moderate oven about 1¹/₄ hours or until tender. Remove pork; keep warm.

2 Strain cooking liquid; reserve liquid. Discard vegetables.

3 Serve pork with sage sauce, roasted tomatoes and potatoes, if desired.

fresh sage sauce Bring reserved liquid to a boil in medium saucepan; whisk in blended butter and flour. Boil, whisking constantly, until thickened slightly; stir in sage.

serves 6

per serving 35.6g fat; 2052kJ
tips Ask your butcher to remove rind and tie pork well.
Roast salted rind on rack in hot oven until crisp; serve with the pork.

meatballs with chilli mushroom sauce

PREPARATION TIME 15 MINUTES ■ COOKING TIME 20 MINUTES

500g pork and veal mince

1 cup (70g) stale breadcrumbs

¼ cup finely chopped fresh oregano

3 cloves garlic, crushed

⅓ cup (95g) tomato paste

1 egg, beaten lightly

1 tablespoon olive oil

**250g button mushrooms,
  sliced thinly**

850g canned tomatoes

¼ cup (60ml) mild chilli sauce

1 Combine mince, breadcrumbs, oregano, garlic, paste and egg in medium bowl; roll level tablespoons of mixture into balls. Place meatballs on oiled oven tray; bake, uncovered, in moderately hot oven about 15 minutes or until cooked through.

2 Meanwhile, heat oil in large saucepan; cook mushrooms, stirring, until just soft. Add undrained crushed tomatoes and sauce to pan; bring to a boil. Reduce heat; simmer, uncovered, 5 minutes. Add meatballs; cook, stirring, 2 minutes.

serves 4

per serving   16.4g fat; 1649kJ

store Recipe can be made 2 days ahead and refrigerated, covered, or frozen for up to 3 months.

pot roast lamb calabrese with creamed polenta

PREPARATION TIME 10 MINUTES ■ COOKING TIME 2 HOURS

2 medium red capsicums (400g)

2 medium yellow capsicums (400g)

1/4 cup (60ml) olive oil

1.5kg lamb neck fillet roasts

2 medium onions (300g), sliced thickly

3 cloves garlic, crushed

425g canned tomatoes

1 cup (250ml) dry red wine

2 tablespoons lamb or chicken stock

2 tablespoons tomato paste

1 tablespoon finely chopped fresh oregano

creamed polenta

1.25 litres (5 cups) water

1 1/4 cups (250g) polenta

50g butter

1/2 cup (40g) coarsely grated parmesan cheese

3/4 cup (180ml) cream

1/4 cup (60ml) chicken stock

1 Halve capsicums; remove and discard seeds and membranes. Cut each half into four equal-sized slices.

2 Heat half of the oil in large frying pan; cook lamb, in batches, until browned lightly. Heat remaining oil in pan; cook onion, garlic and capsicum, stirring, until onion is soft.

3 Return lamb to pan with undrained crushed tomatoes and remaining ingredients; bring to a boil. Reduce heat; simmer, covered, 1 1/2 hours. Uncover; simmer further 1 hour. Remove lamb from pan. Remove and discard string; cover lamb to keep warm.

4 Bring tomato mixture in pan to a boil; reduce heat. Simmer, uncovered, about 20 minutes or until tomato mixture thickens. Return lamb to pan. *[Can be made 2 days ahead to this stage and refrigerated, covered.]*

5 Serve lamb and tomato mixture with creamed polenta.

creamed polenta Bring the water to a boil in large saucepan; reduce heat. Gradually whisk in polenta; cook, stirring, over medium heat, 30 minutes. Stir in remaining ingredients until heated through; serve immediately.

serves 6

per serving 41.5g fat; 3367kJ

tip Lamb neck fillet roasts have to be ordered from your butcher; ask that the lamb be tied securely.

osso buco

Meaning 'hollow bones', osso buco is served throughout Italy but is a specialty of Milan.

90g butter

2 medium carrots (240g), chopped finely

2 large brown onions (400g), chopped finely

3 trimmed sticks celery (225g), chopped finely

2 cloves garlic, crushed

16 pieces veal shin or osso buco (2kg)

plain flour

2 tablespoons olive oil

820g canned tomatoes

1/2 cup (125ml) dry red wine

1 3/4 cups (430ml) beef stock

1 tablespoon finely chopped fresh basil

1 teaspoon finely chopped fresh thyme

1 bay leaf

2.5cm strip lemon rind

1/4 cup finely chopped fresh parsley

1 teaspoon grated lemon rind

1 Heat a third of the butter (30g) in large saucepan; cook carrot, onion, celery and half of the garlic until onion is golden brown. Remove from heat; transfer vegetables to large ovenproof dish.

2 Coat veal with flour. Heat remaining butter and oil in pan. Add veal; brown well each side. Carefully pack veal on top of vegetables.

3 Drain away fat from pan. Add undrained crushed tomatoes, wine, stock, basil, thyme, bay leaf and strip of lemon rind; bring sauce to a boil.

4 Pour sauce over veal. Cover casserole; bake in moderate oven about 1 1/2 hours or until veal is very tender, stirring occasionally. To serve, sprinkle with combined remaining garlic, parsley and grated lemon rind.

serves 6

per serving 9.6g fat; 1695kJ

tip The traditional accompaniment for osso buco is risotto milanese (page 105).

pepper steaks with balsamic browned onion

PREPARATION TIME 10 MINUTES ■ COOKING TIME 20 MINUTES

1 teaspoon cracked black pepper

2 tablespoons finely chopped fresh parsley

4 beef sirloin steaks (800g)

¼ cup (60ml) olive oil

2 large onions (400g), sliced thinly

2 tablespoons balsamic vinegar

1 tablespoon drained, chopped sun-dried tomatoes in oil

2 cloves garlic, crushed

1 Press pepper and parsley onto beef; stand, covered, while cooking onions.

2 Heat 1 tablespoon of the oil in large frying pan; cook onions, stirring, about 10 minutes or until just browned. Add 1 tablespoon of the vinegar; cook, stirring, further 5 minutes or until onion caramelises. Remove from pan; cover to keep warm. Combine remaining oil and vinegar in small screw-top jar with tomatoes and garlic; shake well.

3 Cook beef on heated oiled grill plate (or grill or barbecue) until browned both sides and cooked as desired. Serve beef with browned onions and tomato dressing.

serves 4

per serving 28g fat; 1887kJ

braciole with cheese

PREPARATION TIME 30 MINUTES ■ COOKING TIME 1 HOUR 45 MINUTES

8 beef minute steaks (1.2kg)

4 cloves garlic, crushed

8 slices prosciutto (120g)

200g smoked provolone, cut into 8 slices

3/4 cup (50g) stale breadcrumbs

plain flour

1/4 cup (60ml) olive oil

1 medium white onion (150g), sliced thinly

425g canned tomatoes

1 cup (250ml) water

2 tablespoons tomato paste

1/4 cup (60ml) red wine

1 Place beef out flat on clean surface. Spread garlic over each piece. Top each with a slice of prosciutto and a slice of cheese. Place 1 tablespoon of the breadcrumbs in centre of each piece. Roll up beef to enclose filling; secure with string. Toss rolls in flour; shake away excess.

2 Heat oil in large saucepan; cook beef rolls until well browned all over. Remove from pan. Cook onion in same pan, over low heat until very soft. Stir in undrained crushed tomatoes, the water, paste and wine. Bring to a boil; reduce heat. Simmer, covered, 20 minutes.

3 Remove lid; remove beef rolls to pan. Simmer, uncovered, 15 minutes or until sauce thickens slightly. Remove string before serving.

serves 4

per serving 48.6g fat; 3571kJ

store Recipe best made a day ahead; can be refrigerated, covered, up to 3 days, or frozen for up to 3 months. Reheat in moderately slow oven about 45 minutes or until hot.

rib eye steak
with roasted vegetables

PREPARATION TIME 10 MINUTES ■ COOKING TIME 1 HOUR 20 MINUTES

Beef rib eye is also known as Scotch fillet.

2 medium red capsicums (400g)
2 small eggplants (460g)
2 medium zucchini (240g)
6 beef rib eye steaks (1.3kg)
2 tablespoons olive oil
1/3 cup (60ml) olive paste

1 Quarter capsicums; remove and discard seeds and membranes. Roast capsicum under grill or in very hot oven, skin side up, until skin blisters and blackens. Cover capsicum pieces in plastic or paper 5 minutes. Peel away skin; slice thickly. Cut eggplants into 2cm slices. Cut zucchini, lengthways, into 2cm slices.

2 Cook steaks, in batches, on heated oiled grill plate (or grill or barbecue) until browned both sides and cooked as desired. Cover to keep warm. Heat oil on grill plate; cook capsicum, eggplant and zucchini, in batches, until browned all over and soft.

3 Top steaks with capsicum, eggplant, zucchini and olive paste; drizzle with a little extra olive oil, if desired.

serves 6

per serving 21.8g fat; 1703kJ
tip Recipe best made just before serving.

pork steaks with baked capsicum salad

PREPARATION TIME 20 MINUTES ■ COOKING TIME 1 HOUR 10 MINUTES

4 pork butterfly steaks (600g)

1/2 teaspoon cracked black pepper

1/2 teaspoon dried oregano

2 teaspoons olive oil

1 teaspoon cornflour

1 cup (250ml) chicken stock

2 teaspoons red wine vinegar

baked capsicum salad

2 medium yellow capsicums (400g)

2 large egg tomatoes (180g), halved

90g button mushrooms, sliced thinly

4 cloves garlic, crushed

1/4 teaspoon dried oregano

2 teaspoons olive oil

16 seeded black olives (80g)

2 tablespoons grated parmesan cheese

1 Sprinkle pork with pepper and oregano. Heat oil in large frying pan; cook pork, until tender, turning once. Remove from pan.

2 Add blended cornflour and stock to pan; stir until mixture boils and thickens. Add vinegar; return pork to pan. Turn to coat in sauce.

3 Serve with baked capsicum salad. Sprinkle with fresh oregano, if desired.

baked capsicum salad Quarter capsicums; remove seeds and membranes. Place capsicum on oiled oven tray with tomato, mushrooms and garlic; sprinkle with oregano and oil. Bake, uncovered, in moderately hot oven 40 minutes. Add olives; sprinkle cheese over tomato. Bake further 15 minutes or until capsicum is tender.

serves 4

per serving 11.7g fat; 1239kJ

store Recipe can be made a day ahead and refrigerated, covered.

calves liver with lemon and capers

PREPARATION TIME 10 MINUTES ■ COOKING TIME 10 MINUTES

500g calves liver

1 tablespoon olive oil

60g butter

¼ cup (60ml) lemon juice

½ teaspoon sugar

1 tablespoon baby capers

1 tablespoon fresh flat-leaf parsley leaves

1 Slice liver thinly; remove any membrane.

2 Heat oil and half of the butter in large frying pan. Cook liver quickly, over high heat, until browned all over and cooked as desired; remove from pan.

3 Add juice, sugar and remaining butter to pan; stir over medium heat until butter melts. Return liver to pan with capers and parsley. Cook, turning liver, until well coated and heated through.

serves 4

per serving 27.6g fat; 1538kJ

tip Ask your butcher to slice the liver thinly for you.

veal parmesan

PREPARATION TIME 35 MINUTES ■ COOKING TIME 1 HOUR 20 MINUTES

4 veal steaks (320g)

plain flour

1 egg

1 tablespoon water

packaged breadcrumbs

30g butter

⅓ cup (80ml) olive oil

**2½ cups (250g) grated
mozzarella cheese**

¾ cup (60g) grated parmesan cheese

tomato sauce

1 tablespoon olive oil

**1 medium brown onion (150g),
chopped finely**

**1 trimmed stick celery (75g),
chopped finely**

**1 medium red capsicum (200g),
chopped finely**

1 clove garlic, crushed

410g canned tomatoes

2 teaspoons sugar

1 tablespoon tomato paste

1½ cups (375ml) chicken stock

**1 tablespoon finely chopped
fresh parsley**

**1 tablespoon finely chopped
fresh basil**

1 Pound veal out thinly. Toss veal in flour; shake off excess. Dip in combined beaten egg and water; press on breadcrumbs. Refrigerate veal while preparing tomato sauce.

2 Heat butter and half of the oil in large frying pan; cook veal until browned both sides. Place in ovenproof dish; top veal with mozzarella. Spoon tomato sauce over mozzarella.

3 Sprinkle evenly with parmesan; drizzle with remaining oil. Bake uncovered in moderate oven about 20 minutes or until golden brown.

tomato sauce Heat oil in medium frying pan; cook onion, celery, capsicum and garlic, stirring until onion is soft. Push tomatoes with their liquid through sieve. Add pureed tomato to pan with sugar, paste and stock. Cover; bring to a boil. Reduce heat; simmer, covered, 30 minutes. Remove lid; simmer until sauce is thick. Stir through parsley and basil.

serves 4

per serving 52.8g fat; 3316kJ

poultry and game

Plentiful and inexpensive, chicken is as popular in Italy as it is in the rest of the world. But whether it is pan-fried with a simple sauce or transformed to melting tenderness in a country-style casserole, the flavours are still uniquely Italian. We've also included recipes for quail, duck and rabbit as these robust dishes, of largely peasant origin, are also widely popular.

chicken osso buco

PREPARATION TIME 25 MINUTES ■ COOKING TIME 1 HOUR 45 MINUTES

8 chicken thigh cutlets (1.3kg)

1/4 cup (35g) plain flour

2 tablespoons olive oil

1 large leek (500g), sliced thickly

2 cloves garlic, crushed

2 tablespoons tomato paste

2 1/2 cups (625ml) chicken stock

1/2 cup (125ml) dry white wine

400g canned tomatoes

3 trimmed sticks celery (225g), chopped coarsely

2 medium carrots (240g), chopped coarsely

gremolata

1 medium lemon (140g)

1/4 cup finely chopped fresh parsley

2 cloves garlic, chopped finely

1   Remove and discard skin from chicken. Reserve 1 tablespoon of the flour. Toss chicken in remaining flour; shake off excess. Heat half of the oil in large saucepan; cook chicken, in batches, until browned all over.

2   Heat remaining oil in pan; cook leek and garlic, stirring, until leek is soft. Add reserved flour and paste; cook, stirring, 1 minute. Stir in stock, wine and undrained crushed tomatoes; bring to a boil.

3   Return chicken to pan. Reduce heat; simmer, covered, 1 1/4 hours. Add celery and carrot; simmer, uncovered, 20 minutes or until vegetables are soft. *[Can be made a day ahead to this stage and refrigerated, covered.]*

4   Just before serving, sprinkle with gremolata.

gremolata   Using vegetable peeler, remove rind from lemon. Cut rind into thin strips; chop finely. Combine lemon, parsley and garlic in small bowl; mix well.

serves 4

per serving   15.6g fat; 1971kJ

chicken pancetta casserole

PREPARATION TIME 25 MINUTES ■ COOKING TIME 1 HOUR 20 MINUTES

2kg chicken thigh cutlets

2 tablespoons olive oil

12 slices pancetta (180g)

2 medium brown onions (300g), sliced thinly

2 cloves garlic, crushed

850g canned tomatoes

1/3 cup (95g) tomato paste

1 cup (250ml) dry white wine

2 cups (500ml) chicken stock

2 medium carrots (240g), chopped coarsely

1/3 cup finely chopped fresh flat-leaf parsley

1 Remove and discard skin from chicken.

2 Heat half of the oil in large saucepan; cook chicken, in batches, until browned all over.

3 Cut pancetta slices in half. Heat remaining oil in pan; cook onion, garlic and pancetta, stirring, until pancetta is browned.

4 Return chicken to pan with undrained crushed tomatoes, paste, wine and stock; bring to a boil. Reduce heat; simmer, uncovered, 30 minutes. Add carrot; simmer about 30 minutes or until carrot is tender. *[Can be made a day ahead to this stage and refrigerated, covered, or frozen for up to 2 months.]*

5 Stir through parsley just before serving. Serve with tiny new potatoes, if desired.

serves 8

per serving 20.8g fat; 1682kJ

quail with polenta

PREPARATION TIME 25 MINUTES (plus refrigeration time) ■ COOKING TIME 55 MINUTES

8 quail (1.6kg)

2 teaspoons olive oil

5 slices pancetta (75g), chopped coarsely

1 tablespoon pine nuts

¼ cup (60ml) brandy

¼ cup (40g) raisins

1¾ cups (430ml) chicken stock

marinade

½ cup (125ml) olive oil

1 tablespoon coarsely chopped fresh rosemary

2 teaspoons coarsely chopped fresh thyme

1 tablespoon finely shredded lemon rind

polenta

1½ cups (375ml) chicken stock

½ cup (85g) polenta

30g butter, melted

¼ cup (20g) grated parmesan cheese

2 tablespoons polenta, extra

olive oil for shallow-frying

1 Remove and discard necks from quail. Using kitchen scissors, cut through either side of backbone; discard backbone. Cut quail in half. Rinse quail under cold running water; pat dry with absorbent paper.

2 Place quail in large shallow non-reactive dish. Pour over marinade; refrigerate, covered, 3 hours. *[Can be made a day ahead to this stage.]*

3 Heat oil in large frying pan; cook drained quail, in batches, covered, 5 minutes. Turn quail; cook, covered, further 7 minutes or until well browned and tender. Keep warm in moderate oven.

4 Add pancetta and pine nuts to pan; cook, stirring, 2 minutes or until pine nuts are browned lightly. Add brandy and raisins; cook 2 minutes or until liquid reduces by half. Add stock; simmer, uncovered, about 5 minutes or until thickened slightly.

5 Serve quail with polenta and sauce.

marinade Combine ingredients in small bowl; mix well.

polenta Bring stock to a boil in large saucepan. Gradually add polenta; simmer, stirring, about 10 minutes or until soft and thick. Stir in butter and cheese. Press firmly into oiled 17cm sandwich cake pan; cool. Refrigerate, covered, 3 hours. *[Can be made a day ahead to this stage.]* Turn cooked polenta out of pan; cut into wedges. Coat wedges in extra polenta. Heat oil in medium frying pan; shallow-fry polenta wedges until browned lightly.

serves 4

per serving 87.7g fat; 4867kJ

chicken, lemon and artichoke skewers

PREPARATION TIME 20 MINUTES ■ COOKING TIME 10 MINUTES

3 medium lemons (420g)

2 cloves garlic, crushed

¼ cup (60ml) olive oil

600g chicken breast fillets, chopped coarsely

800g canned artichoke hearts, drained, halved

24 button mushrooms

1 Squeeze juice from one lemon (you will need two tablespoons of juice). Combine juice, garlic and oil in small screw-top jar; shake well.

2 Cut remaining lemons into 24 wedges. Thread chicken, artichoke, mushrooms and lemon onto 12 skewers. *[Can be made a day ahead to this stage and refrigerated, covered.]*

3 Cook skewers on heated oiled grill plate (or grill or barbecue) until browned all over and cooked through. Brush with oil mixture during cooking.

serves 4

per serving 22.6g fat; 1534kJ

chicken marsala

PREPARATION TIME 15 MINUTES ■ COOKING TIME 15 MINUTES

60g butter

1 clove garlic, crushed

4 single chicken breast fillets (680g)

4 slices mozzarella cheese

12 capers, drained

4 anchovy fillets, drained

1 tablespoon finely chopped fresh parsley

1/4 cup (60ml) marsala

2/3 cup (160ml) cream

1 Melt butter in large frying pan. Cook garlic and chicken until browned both sides; remove from pan. Arrange one slice of the cheese, three capers and one anchovy fillet on each chicken fillet; sprinkle with parsley.

2 Return chicken to pan; cover. Cook over moderate heat until chicken is cooked through; remove from pan. Place on serving dish; keep warm.

3 Add marsala to pan; scrape brown bits off bottom of pan. Reduce heat; add cream. Simmer gently, uncovered, a few minutes until sauce thickens. Spoon sauce over chicken.

serves 4

per serving 44.8g fat; 2583kJ

chicken cacciatore

PREPARATION TIME 30 MINUTES ■ COOKING TIME 1 HOUR 20 MINUTES

2 tablespoons olive oil

1.5kg chicken pieces

1 medium brown onion (150g), chopped finely

1 clove garlic, crushed

1/2 cup (125ml) dry white wine

1 1/2 tablespoons vinegar

1/2 cup (125ml) chicken stock

410g canned tomatoes

1 tablespoon tomato paste

1 teaspoon finely chopped fresh basil

1 teaspoon sugar

3 anchovy fillets, chopped finely

1/4 cup (60ml) milk

60g seeded black olives, halved

1 tablespoon finely chopped fresh parsley

1 Heat oil in large frying pan; cook chicken until browned all over.
   Place chicken in ovenproof dish.

2 Pour off most pan juices, leaving about 1 tablespoon in pan. Add
   onion and garlic to pan; cook until onion is soft. Add wine and
   vinegar; bring to a boil. Boil until reduced by half. Add stock; stir over
   high heat 2 minutes. Push tomatoes with their liquid through sieve;
   add to pan with paste, basil and sugar. Cook further 1 minute.

3 Pour tomato mixture over chicken pieces. Cover; cook in moderate
   oven 1 hour.

4 Soak anchovy in milk 5 minutes; drain on absorbent paper. Arrange
   chicken pieces on serving dish; keep warm. Pour pan juices into
   medium saucepan. Bring to a boil; boil 1 minute. Add anchovy, olives
   and parsley to pan; cook 1 minute. Pour sauce over chicken pieces.
   Sprinkle with extra chopped parsley, if desired.

serves 4

per serving 42.2g fat; 2572kJ

rabbit with rosemary and white wine

PREPARATION TIME 20 MINUTES ■ COOKING TIME 2 HOURS 10 MINUTES

2 rabbits (2kg)

¼ cup (60ml) olive oil

1 medium leek (350g), sliced thinly

2 trimmed sticks celery (150g), chopped finely

2 cloves garlic, crushed

¼ cup (35g) plain flour

2½ cups (625ml) chicken stock

½ cup (125ml) dry white wine

1 tablespoon fresh rosemary

200g button mushrooms

2 medium zucchini (240g), sliced thinly

1 tablespoon finely chopped fresh parsley

1 Clean and trim rabbits; cut into pieces. Rinse under cold water; pat dry with absorbent paper.

2 Heat 1 tablespoon of the oil in large frying pan. Cook rabbit, in batches, until browned all over; drain on absorbent paper. Heat remaining oil in pan; cook leek, celery and garlic, stirring, until leek is soft.

3 Stir in flour; stir until mixture is dry and grainy. Remove pan from heat; gradually stir in stock and wine. Stir over heat until mixture boils and thickens. Return rabbit to pan; add rosemary. Simmer, covered, about 1½ hours or until rabbit is tender.

4 Add vegetables; simmer, covered, 20 minutes or until vegetables are tender. Stir in parsley.

serves 4

per serving 32g fat; 3580kJ

store Recipe can be made a day ahead and refrigerated, covered, or frozen for up to 3 months.

chicken parmesan with basil dressing

PREPARATION TIME 25 MINUTES ■ COOKING TIME 20 MINUTES

2 cups (140g) stale breadcrumbs

**1/3 cup (25g) finely grated
parmesan cheese**

**2 tablespoons finely chopped fresh
flat-leaf parsley**

12 chicken tenderloins (750g)

3/4 cup (110g) plain flour

2 eggs, beaten lightly

250g curly endive

150g rocket

basil dressing

1 cup firmly packed fresh basil

1/2 cup (125ml) olive oil

1/4 cup (60ml) lemon juice

1 clove garlic, crushed

1 Combine breadcrumbs, cheese and parsley in medium bowl.

2 Toss chicken in flour to coat; shake away excess. Dip in egg, then in breadcrumb mixture to coat. Place on oiled oven trays. *[Can be made a day ahead to this stage and refrigerated, covered, or frozen for up to 2 months.]*

3 Bake in moderately hot oven, uncovered, about 20 minutes or until browned lightly and cooked through.

4 Serve chicken with endive and rocket; drizzle with basil dressing.

basil dressing Blend or process ingredients until combined. *[Can be made a day ahead and refrigerated, covered.]*

serves 4

per serving 43.8g fat; 3162kJ

tips Make breadcrumbs from any stale bread (sourdough or ciabatta are both good).
When blending or processing bread to make breadcrumbs, add parmesan and parsley at the very end of processing time, pulsing just a few times to combine the three ingredients thoroughly.

slow-roasted duck
with sage and rosemary

PREPARATION TIME 30 MINUTES ■ COOKING TIME 4 HOURS

**2 tablespoons finely chopped
fresh sage**

**2 tablespoons finely chopped
fresh rosemary**

2 teaspoons salt

6 cloves garlic, crushed

2 tablespoons olive oil

1.6kg duck

**3 medium white onions (450g),
chopped coarsely**

**2 medium carrots (240g),
chopped coarsely**

**3 medium tomatoes (380g),
chopped coarsely**

1 cup (250ml) red wine

1/2 cup (125ml) chicken stock

1 Combine herbs, salt, garlic and half of the oil in small bowl.

2 Wash duck under cold running water; remove and discard fat from inside cavity. Pat duck dry with absorbent paper. Place half of the onion inside cavity of duck. Loosen skin of duck by sliding fingers between skin and meat at the neck joint; spread half of the herb mixture under skin evenly. Tuck wings under duck; tie legs together with kitchen string.

3 Heat remaining oil in large flameproof baking dish; cook remaining onion, carrot and tomato, stirring, until tomato begins to soften. Add wine and stock to dish; bring to a boil. Remove from heat; stir in remaining herb mixture.

4 Place duck on top of vegetable mixture. Bake tightly covered, in slow oven 3 1/2 hours, basting with juices several times during cooking.

5 Carefully remove duck from dish and place on oven tray. Return to oven; bake, uncovered, about 30 minutes or until skin is crisp and golden.

6 Meanwhile, strain pan contents into medium saucepan; discard vegetables. Blot the top of pan juices with absorbent paper to remove as much fat as possible. Reheat pan juices and serve over duck.

serves 4

per serving 93.8g fat; 4432kJ

tip Serve with creamy whipped potatoes and lots of fresh bread to mop up the sauce.

grandmother's chicken

PREPARATION TIME 15 MINUTES ■ COOKING TIME 1 HOUR 30 MINUTES

2 tablespoons vegetable oil

1 large brown onion (200g), sliced thickly

2 cloves garlic, crushed

4 chicken thigh cutlets (640g)

4 chicken drumsticks (600g)

4 sprigs fresh rosemary

4 medium potatoes (800g), chopped coarsely

2 medium tomatoes (380g), chopped coarsely

½ cup (125ml) chicken stock

150g button mushrooms, halved

4 bacon rashers, chopped coarsely

½ cup (80g) kalamata black olives

1 Heat oil in large flameproof baking dish; cook onion and garlic, stirring, until onion is soft. Add chicken; cook, stirring, until just browned all over. Add rosemary, potato, tomato and stock.

2 Bake, uncovered, in hot oven 1 hour. Stir in mushrooms, bacon and olives. Bake, uncovered, about 20 minutes or until chicken is tender.

serves 4

per serving 45.5g fat; 3117kJ

store Recipe can be made 2 days ahead and refrigerated, covered, or frozen for up to 2 months.

char-grilled chicken with broad beans
and chive butter

PREPARATION TIME 15 MINUTES ■ COOKING TIME 20 MINUTES

750g broad beans, shelled

1 tablespoon olive oil

1 small red onion (100g), sliced thinly

2 cloves garlic, crushed

2 medium tomatoes (380g),
  chopped coarsely

2 tablespoons coarsely chopped
  fresh parsley

4 single chicken breast fillets (680g)

chive butter

60g butter

2 tablespoons fresh chives

1 Boil, steam or microwave beans until tender; cool. Remove and discard grey skins.

2 Heat oil in medium frying pan; cook onion, covered, over low heat until very soft and starting to caramelise. Add garlic and beans; stir until heated through. Stir in tomato and parsley; stir over low heat 5 minutes.

3 Meanwhile, cook chicken on heated oiled grill plate (or grill or barbecue) about 5 minutes or until cooked though; turn once during cooking.

4 Serve chicken on bean mixture; top with chive butter.

chive butter Combine butter and chives in small bowl.

serves 4

per serving 27g fat; 1902kJ

salami, potato and basil frittata

PREPARATION TIME 10 MINUTES
COOKING TIME 45 MINUTES (plus cooling time)

2 medium potatoes (400g), sliced thinly
250g italian salami, chopped finely
6 eggs, beaten lightly
½ cup (125ml) cream
3 green onions, chopped coarsely
1 tablespoon finely shredded fresh basil

1 Grease deep 20cm-round cake pan; line base and side with baking paper.

2 Boil, steam or microwave potato until just tender. Drain; cool.

3 Cook salami in small heated non-stick frying pan, stirring, until salami is browned all over; drain on absorbent paper.

4 Layer half of the potato over base of prepared pan; top with half of the salami. Repeat with remaining potato and salami. Pour in combined egg, cream, onion and basil; bake uncovered, in moderate oven about 30 minutes or until firm. Frittata can be served warm or cold.

serves 4

per serving 45.1g fat; 2388kJ
store Frittata can be made a day ahead and refrigerated, covered.
tip Frittata can be cooked on top of the stove, in a medium lightly oiled high-sided frying pan; cook on low heat, uncovered, until almost set, then brown frittata under a preheated grill.

tuna and asparagus frittata

PREPARATION TIME 10 MINUTES
COOKING TIME 30 MINUTES

5 medium potatoes (1kg), sliced thinly
1 medium brown onion (150g), sliced thinly
1 clove garlic, crushed
250g asparagus, trimmed, chopped coarsely
425g canned tuna, drained
8 eggs, beaten lightly
2 tablespoons finely chopped fresh flat-leaf parsley
cooking-oil spray

1 Boil, steam or microwave potato until almost tender.

2 Cook onion and garlic in small heated non-stick frying pan, stirring, until onion softens.

3 Combine potato and onion mixture in large bowl with asparagus, tuna, egg, and parsley.

4 Reheat pan; remove from heat. Spray lightly with cooking-oil spray; return to heat. Spoon frittata mixture into pan; press down firmly. Cook, uncovered, over low heat until almost set; remove from heat. Place under heated grill until frittata sets and top is browned lightly.

serves 4

per serving 13.9g fat; 1858kJ
store Frittata can be made a day ahead and refrigerated, covered.

rocket and prosciutto frittata

PREPARATION TIME 15 MINUTES
COOKING TIME 35 MINUTES (plus standing time)

8 slices prosciutto (120g)
40g rocket leaves
1/2 cup (20g) finely grated parmesan cheese
10 eggs, beaten lightly
3/4 cup (180ml) cream

1 Grease deep 19cm-square cake pan; line base and two opposite sides with baking paper.

2 Cook prosciutto, in batches, in medium heated non-stick frying pan until browned all over and crisp; drain on absorbent paper.

3 Place half of the prosciutto in prepared pan; cover with half of the rocket then half of the cheese. Repeat with remaining prosciutto, rocket and cheese.

4 Pour combined egg and cream into pan, pressing down on prosciutto mixture to cover completely with egg mixture.

5 Bake, uncovered, in moderate oven about 30 minutes or until firm; stand 5 minutes. Turn out of pan; cut into eight pieces.

serves 4

per serving 25.3g fat; 1373kJ
store Frittata can be made a day ahead and refrigerated, covered.
tip Serve frittata warm or cold.

frittata with onions and zucchini

PREPARATION TIME 10 MINUTES
COOKING TIME 30 MINUTES (plus cooling time)

20g butter, melted
2 tablespoons olive oil
2 medium brown onions (300g), sliced thinly
6 eggs, beaten lightly
1/4 cup (60ml) cream
3/4 cup (60g) grated parmesan cheese
2 small zucchini (180g), sliced thinly
1 tablespoon finely shredded fresh basil

1 Brush base and sides of deep 19cm-square cake pan with butter. Heat oil in medium frying pan. Cook onion, stirring, until soft; cool.

2 Combine onion, egg, cream, cheese, zucchini and basil in medium bowl. Pour mixture into prepared pan; bake, uncovered, in moderate oven about 25 minutes or until browned lightly and firm.

serves 4

per serving 13g fat; 672kJ
store Recipe can be made a day ahead and refrigerated, covered.

salads and vegetables

From artichokes to zucchini, fresh vegetables of some kind are always part of what Italians call *il contorno* or accompaniments. But this suggests a supporting role, while many of the vegetable dishes in this chapter would make light meals in themselves, or a delicious addition to an antipasto platter.

panzanella

½ **loaf stale ciabatta (275g)**
6 **medium tomatoes (1.1kg)**
2 **trimmed sticks celery (150g)**
1 **lebanese cucumber (130g)**
1 **medium red onion (170g)**
¼ **cup (60ml) red wine vinegar**
½ **cup (125ml) olive oil**
1 **clove garlic, crushed**
¼ **cup finely shredded fresh basil**

1 Remove and discard soft centre from ciabatta; cut remaining bread into 2cm cubes.

2 Cut tomatoes into wedges. Discard seeds; chop coarsely.

3 Cut celery into four strips lengthways; chop strips coarsely.

4 Peel cucumber; cut in half lengthways. Discard seeds; cut halves into 5mm-thick slices.

5 Chop onion coarsely; combine with bread cubes, tomato, celery and cucumber in large bowl.

6 Combine remaining ingredients in screw-top jar; shake well. Pour dressing over salad; toss gently.

serves 4

per serving 30.1g fat; 1600kJ
tips Add capers for extra flavour.
Instead of discarding the soft white centre of the bread, you can blend or process it into fine breadcrumbs, or try cutting it into small cubes and toasting until golden brown and crunchy.

artichokes with lemon caper dressing

PREPARATION TIME 20 MINUTES ■ COOKING TIME 45 MINUTES

4 medium artichokes (800g)

½ cup (125ml) lemon juice

½ cup (125ml) light olive oil

2 cloves garlic, crushed

2 tablespoons capers, chopped coarsely

¼ cup coarsely chopped fresh flat-leaf parsley

1 Trim artichoke stalks to 1cm; remove tough outer leaves. Cut off top quarter of remaining leaves. Using small spoon, scoop out centre of artichoke to remove choke; discard.

2 Place artichokes, cut-side down, in steamer. Steam artichokes, covered tightly, about 45 minutes or until stems are tender when tested with a skewer; cut in half. Place hot artichokes on serving plates; drizzle with combined remaining ingredients.

serves 4

per serving 30g fat; 1300kJ

grilled vegetables
with balsamic dressing

PREPARATION TIME 15 MINUTES ■ COOKING TIME 20 MINUTES

2 medium green capsicums (400g)

2 medium red capsicums (400g)

2 medium yellow capsicums (400g)

1 large red onion (300g)

2 medium green zucchini (240g)

2 medium yellow zucchini (240g)

6 baby eggplants (360g)

balsamic dressing

2 tablespoons lemon juice

1 clove garlic, crushed

¼ cup (60ml) olive oil

2 tablespoons balsamic vinegar

1 tablespoon coarsely chopped fresh oregano

1   Quarter capsicums; remove and discard seeds and membranes. Cut into thick strips. Cut onion into eight wedges.

2   Cut zucchini and eggplants lengthways into thin slices.

3   Cook vegetables, in batches, on heated oiled grill plate (or grill or barbecue) until browned all over and tender. Combine vegetables in large bowl. Drizzle with balsamic dressing; mix well.

balsamic dressing   Combine ingredients in screw-top jar; shake well.

[Can be made a week ahead and refrigerated, covered.]

serves 6

per serving   10.2g fat; 637kJ

store   Salad is best made a day ahead to infuse grilled vegetables with the flavour of the dressing.

radicchio and fennel salad

PREPARATION TIME 20 MINUTES

1 radicchio lettuce

2 medium fennel bulbs (1kg), cut into 1cm strips

100g seeded black olives

½ cup firmly packed fresh parsley

dressing

¼ cup (60ml) olive oil

1 tablespoon lemon juice

2 anchovy fillets

3 seeded black olives

1 clove garlic, crushed

1 Separate lettuce leaves; wash thoroughly.

2 Arrange lettuce, fennel, olives and parsley on plate. Spoon dressing over salad.

dressing Blend or process ingredients 10 seconds.

serves 4

per serving 14.5g fat; 830kJ

peperonata

PREPARATION TIME 15 MINUTES ■ COOKING TIME 35 MINUTES

2 medium red capsicums (400g)

2 medium yellow capsicums (400g)

2 medium green capsicums (400g)

2 tablespoons olive oil

3 medium onions (450g), sliced thinly

2 cloves garlic, crushed

2 large tomatoes (500g), seeded, chopped coarsely

¼ cup (60ml) dry white wine

½ cup pimiento-stuffed green olives (60g), chopped coarsely

1 tablespoon coarsely chopped fresh flat-leaf parsley

1 Halve capsicums; remove and discard seeds and membranes. Cut capsicums into thin strips.

2 Heat oil in large frying pan; cook onion and garlic, stirring, until onion is soft. Stir in capsicums and tomato; simmer, covered, about 30 minutes or until capsicums are soft, stirring occasionally.

3 Stir in wine and olives; simmer, uncovered, about 5 minutes or until liquid evaporates. Stir in parsley; serve peperonata hot or cold.

serves 6

per serving 6.7g fat; 597kJ

store Recipe can be made 3 days ahead and refrigerated, covered.

capsicums
with tomato anchovy filling

PREPARATION TIME 20 MINUTES ■ COOKING TIME 45 MINUTES

2 tablespoons olive oil
1 medium brown onion (150g), chopped finely
1 clove garlic, crushed
½ small eggplant (115g), chopped finely
1 tablespoon coarsely chopped fresh flat-leaf parsley
1 tablespoon coarsely chopped fresh oregano
2 teaspoons drained capers, chopped coarsely
4 drained anchovy fillets, chopped finely
4 medium egg tomatoes (300g), chopped finely
¼ cup (15g) stale breadcrumbs
¼ cup (20g) grated parmesan cheese
2 medium red capsicums (400g)

1 Heat half of the oil in large saucepan; cook onion and garlic, stirring, until onion is soft. Stir in eggplant, herbs, capers, anchovy and tomato; cook, stirring, 3 minutes. Transfer mixture to large bowl; cool.

2 Stir in breadcrumbs and cheese.

3 Cut capsicums in half lengthways; remove seeds and membranes. Brush skin with remaining oil; place capsicum on oven tray. Fill capsicum with tomato mixture; bake, uncovered, in moderate oven about 40 minutes or until capsicums are tender.

serves 4

per serving 11.6g fat; 724kJ
tip Recipe can be prepared a day ahead and refrigerated, covered.

roasted tomato and cannellini bean salad

PREPARATION TIME 15 MINUTES (plus soaking time) ■ COOKING TIME 45 MINUTES

2 cups (400g) dried cannellini beans

6 large egg tomatoes (540g), quartered

1/3 cup (80ml) olive oil

1/2 teaspoon cracked black pepper

1 tablespoon finely grated lemon rind

1/4 cup whole fresh basil

1 3/4 cups (210g) seeded black olives, halved

1 clove garlic, crushed

1/3 cup (80ml) lemon juice

1 teaspoon sugar

1 Cover beans with cold water in large bowl. Soak overnight; drain.

2 Cook beans, uncovered, in large saucepan of boiling water, about 45 minutes or until tender. Drain; cool.

3 Meanwhile, place tomato in large baking dish. Drizzle with half of the oil; sprinkle with pepper. Bake, uncovered, in very hot oven about 30 minutes or until soft.

4 Place beans and tomato in large bowl with rind, basil, olives and remaining ingredients; toss gently to combine.

serves 8

per serving 12g fat; 1048kJ

tip 1.2kg of any canned white beans, drained and rinsed, can be substituted for dried cannellini beans in this recipe.

baby rocket and parmesan salad

PREPARATION TIME 25 MINUTES ■ COOKING TIME 3 MINUTES

60g parmesan cheese

200g baby rocket

**80g semi-dried tomatoes,
    halved lengthways**

¼ cup pine nuts (40g), toasted

¼ cup (60ml) balsamic vinegar

¼ cup (60ml) extra virgin olive oil

1 Using vegetable peeler, shave cheese into wide, long pieces.

2 Combine rocket with tomato and nuts in large bowl; add cheese. Drizzle with combined vinegar and oil; toss gently.

serves 8

per serving 16g fat; 744kJ

tips Baby spinach can be substituted for rocket. To keep rocket crisp, rinse under cold water; place in airtight plastic bag and refrigerate several hours or overnight.

Nuts of any kind can be toasted on top of stove in a dry heavy-based frying pan, stirring, over medium heat, until they are just golden brown.

gorgonzola fritters

PREPARATION TIME 15 MINUTES (plus standing time)
COOKING TIME 5 MINUTES

- 1 cup (200g) ricotta cheese
- 1 cup (185g) gorgonzola cheese, chopped coarsely
- 2 eggs, beaten lightly
- ½ cup (75g) plain flour
- vegetable oil for deep-frying
- 1 cup (80g) finely grated parmesan cheese

1 Combine ricotta, gorgonzola and egg in medium bowl. Whisk in flour; stand at room temperature 1 hour. *[Can be made a day ahead to this stage and refrigerated, covered.]*

2 Heat oil in large saucepan; deep-fry heaped teaspoons of mixture, turning occasionally, until fritters are browned lightly all over and cooked through. Do not have oil too hot or fritters will over-brown before cooking through. Place parmesan in medium bowl; toss fritters, in batches, to coat as they are cooked.

makes 36

per serving 4g fat; 231kJ
tip Gorgonzola is a creamy blue cheese from Italy; if unavailable use blue castello or a similar soft blue cheese.

marinated bocconcini

PREPARATION TIME 5 MINUTES

- 500g bocconcini cheese, quartered
- 6 whole black peppercorns
- 3 bay leaves
- 3 sprigs fresh rosemary
- 3 sprigs fresh oregano
- ¼ cup (60ml) white wine vinegar
- 2 cups (500ml) olive oil, approximately

1 Combine cheese, peppercorns, bay leaves, rosemary and oregano in large bowl. Transfer to large sterilised 1-litre (4 cup) jar.

2 Pour vinegar over cheese mixture in jar. Add enough of the oil to cover completely; seal. Refrigerate at least 6 hours.

serves 6

per serving 23.6g fat; 1124kJ
store Recipe can be refrigerated 2 weeks.
tip Marinated bocconcini makes a great addition to antipasto platters or fresh green salads; use baby bocconcini, if available.

herbed baked ricotta

PREPARATION TIME 15 MINUTES
COOKING TIME 1 HOUR (plus cooling time)

1kg ricotta cheese
2 tablespoons finely chopped fresh thyme
2 cloves garlic, crushed
2 eggs, beaten lightly
1 tablespoon finely chopped garlic chives
1 tablespoon finely grated lemon rind

1 Grease deep 20cm-round cake pan; line base
with baking paper.

2 Place cheese in large bowl with thyme, garlic,
egg, chives and rind; stir until well combined.
Spoon cheese mixture into prepared pan.

3 Bake, uncovered, in moderate oven about
1 hour or until browned lightly and firm to touch;
cool in pan.

serves 8

per serving 35.7g fat; 1943kJ
store Recipe can be refrigerated, covered, 3 days.
tip Try adding a few tablespoons of finely chopped
pancetta or black olives to ricotta mixture before baking.

parmesan crisps

PREPARATION TIME 5 MINUTES
COOKING TIME 25 MINUTES

1 cup (80g) finely grated parmesan cheese
¼ teaspoon finely ground black pepper
1 teaspoon dried oregano

1 Combine ingredients in medium bowl. Place
2 teaspoons of mixture, 3cm apart, on baking
paper lined oven trays; flatten with fingertips.

2 Bake, uncovered, in moderately hot oven
4 minutes; cool on trays.

makes 18

per serving 1.4g fat; 82kJ
store Crisps can be made 3 days ahead and stored in an
airtight container.
tip Although these crisps make a great snack on their own,
you can also use them to accompany dips or soup. Make
crisps in two large sheets, then break into shards to serve. The
flavourings can be omitted and the plain crisps topped with
olive paste and a little sour cream for finger food.

cheese

desserts

While the preferred finish to an Italian meal is fruit, when a
special occasion demands a special dessert, Italians can
produce the most luscious, creamy concoctions imaginable,
as well as refreshing fruit-based granita and gelato.

zabaglione

PREPARATION TIME 10 MINUTES ■ COOKING TIME 10 MINUTES

5 egg yolks
¼ cup (55g) caster sugar
½ cup (125ml) sweet marsala
¼ cup (60ml) dry white wine

1 Beat yolks and sugar in medium heatproof bowl with electric mixer until well combined.

2 Place bowl of mixture over medium saucepan of simmering water. Gradually beat in half of the marsala and half of the white wine; beat well. Gradually beat in remaining marsala and wine.

3 Beat constantly, about 10 minutes, or until thick and creamy. If mixture adheres to side of bowl, quickly remove from heat and beat vigorously with wooden spoon – especially around base. Pour into individual dishes; serve immediately.

serves 4

per serving 7.7g fat; 1160kJ
tip Zabaglione makes an excellent topping for fresh fruit.

lemon gelato

PREPARATION TIME 15 MINUTES (plus freezing time) ■ COOKING TIME 15 MINUTES (plus cooling time)

½ cup (110g) caster sugar

½ cup (125ml) water

½ cup (125ml) sweet or dry white wine

½ cup (125ml) lemon juice, strained

1 egg white

1 Combine sugar, the water and wine in small saucepan; stir over low heat until sugar dissolves. Bring to a boil; reduce heat. Simmer, uncovered, 10 minutes; cool. Stir in juice; mix well. Pour into lamington pan; freeze, covered, until mixture is just firm.

2 Remove from freezer. Turn mixture into medium bowl; beat until smooth with fork. Beat egg white in small bowl with electric mixer until firm; fold into lemon mixture. Return to pan; freeze until firm.

serves 2

per serving 0.13g fat; 1155kJ

store Gelato is best made a day ahead and can be frozen, covered for up to 3 days.

fresh fig
and mascarpone tartlets

PREPARATION TIME 35 MINUTES (plus refrigeration time) ■ COOKING TIME 40 MINUTES

1 cup (150g) plain flour
1 tablespoon custard powder
1 tablespoon caster sugar
100g butter, chopped coarsely
1 egg yolk
1 teaspoon grated orange rind
2 teaspoons water, approximately
2 large fresh figs (160g)

toffee

1¼ cups (275g) caster sugar
½ cup (125ml) water
**¼ cup (40g) blanched
    almonds, toasted**
½ cup (125ml) strained orange juice
2 tablespoons water, extra

mascarpone cream

½ cup (125ml) thickened cream
200g mascarpone cheese

1 Grease four deep 10cm-round loose-based flan tins. Place flour, custard powder and sugar into medium bowl; rub in butter. Stir in yolk, rind and enough of the water to mix to a soft dough. Knead dough on floured surface until smooth; refrigerate, covered, 1 hour.

2 Roll pastry between sheets of baking paper until large enough to line prepared tins; lift pastry into tins. Press into sides; trim edges. Place tins on oven tray; prick bases with fork. Cover pastry with baking paper; fill with dried beans or rice. Bake, uncovered, in moderate oven 10 minutes. Remove paper and beans. Bake, uncovered, further 10 minutes or until browned lightly; cool. *[Can be made 3 days ahead and stored in airtight container.]*

3 Halve figs; cut each half into three wedges, ready for dipping in toffee.

4 Place pastry cases on serving plates; fill with mascarpone cream. Top each with toffee-coated fig wedges and toffee strands; pour warm orange syrup around tartlets.

toffee Cover three oven trays with foil. Combine sugar and the water in small saucepan; stir over heat, without boiling, until sugar dissolves. Simmer, uncovered, without stirring, until mixture turns golden brown; remove from heat. Dip fig wedges into toffee; place on one oven tray to set. Place nuts on another oven tray; pour over half of the remaining toffee. Stand until set; break almond toffee into pieces, then blend or process until crushed finely. Gently reheat remaining toffee; working quickly, dip fork into pan and drizzle long thin strands of toffee onto remaining oven tray. Add juice and the extra water to any toffee remaining in pan; simmer about 5 minutes or until mixture is syrupy.

mascarpone cream Whip cream in small bowl until firm peaks form; fold in mascarpone, in two batches, then finely crushed almond toffee.

serves 4

per serving 68.2g fat; 3431kJ

watermelon granita with gingered pineapple

PREPARATION TIME 30 MINUTES ■ COOKING TIME 30 MINUTES (plus cooling, freezing and refrigeration time)

2kg watermelon, chopped coarsely
¾ cup (165g) sugar
2 cups (500ml) water
4 egg whites

gingered pineapple
50g piece fresh ginger, sliced thinly
¼ cup (60ml) green ginger wine
½ cup (110g) sugar
3 cups (750ml) water
1 small pineapple (800g), chopped coarsely
1 tablespoon finely chopped fresh mint

1 Blend or process watermelon until pureed; push through sieve into large bowl. Discard seeds and pulp; reserve juice.

2 Combine sugar and the water in medium saucepan; stir over low heat until sugar dissolves. Bring to a boil; reduce heat. Simmer, uncovered, without stirring, 10 minutes; cool.

3 Pour sugar syrup into bowl with watermelon juice; stir to combine. Pour granita mixture into 20cm x 30cm lamington pan. Cover with foil; freeze about 3 hours or until just set.

4 Remove granita mixture from freezer and place in large bowl with egg whites; beat with electric mixer until smooth. Pour into 14cm x 21cm loaf pan. Cover; freeze overnight or until frozen.

5 Serve granita with gingered pineapple.

gingered pineapple Combine ginger, wine, sugar and the water in large saucepan; stir over low heat until sugar dissolves. Bring to a boil; reduce heat. Simmer, uncovered, without stirring, 10 minutes. Pour syrup into large heatproof bowl. Add pineapple; cool. Cover; refrigerate 3 hours. *[Can be made a day ahead to this stage.]* Just before serving, stir in mint.

serves 6

per serving 0.5g fat; 1136kJ
store Recipe must be made several hours before serving.
tip Honeydew melon can be substituted for the watermelon.

tiramisu

PREPARATION TIME 25 MINUTES

2 tablespoons instant coffee
1¼ cups (310ml) boiling water
1 cup (250ml) sweet marsala
250g packet sponge-finger biscuits
½ cup (125ml) thickened cream
⅓ cup (55g) icing sugar
2 cups (500g) mascarpone cheese
40g dark chocolate, grated
125g blueberries

1 Dissolve coffee in the water in medium bowl. Stir in ⅔ cup (160ml) of the marsala; cool. Dip half of the biscuits, one at a time, in coffee mixture; arrange in single layer, in 2.5-litre (10 cup) glass dish.

2 Beat cream and icing sugar in small bowl until soft peaks form; fold in the mascarpone and remaining marsala.

3 Spread half of the cream mixture over biscuits in dish. Dip remaining biscuits in remaining coffee mixture; arrange on top of cream layer. Top biscuit layer with remaining cream mixture; sprinkle with chocolate. Cover; refrigerate several hours. *[Can be made 2 days ahead to this stage and refrigerated, covered.]*

4 Decorate top with blueberries, just before serving.

serves 6

per serving 59.5g fat; 3628kJ

tips As with most desserts containing syrup, the flavour will develop more if made a day ahead and refrigerated, covered.
Any type of berries are suitable for this recipe.

ricotta cake

PREPARATION TIME 1 HOUR ■ COOKING TIME 1 HOUR (plus cooling time)

370g packet chocolate cake mix
185g ricotta cheese
1/4 cup (55g) caster sugar
2 tablespoons Grand Marnier
30g glacé ginger, chopped finely
30g glacé cherries, chopped finely
30g dark chocolate, chopped finely
90g flaked almonds, toasted

syrup
2 tablespoons caster sugar
1/3 cup (80ml) water
2 tablespoons Grand Marnier

icing
1/4 cup (55g) caster sugar
1/3 cup (80ml) water
125g butter
90g dark chocolate, melted

1 Make up cake mix according to directions on packet; spoon mixture into greased 23cm-round cake pan. Bake in moderate oven about 25 minutes or until cake is cooked when tested; turn onto wire rack to cool.

2 Push cheese through wire sieve into small bowl; beat with electric mixer until smooth and creamy. With motor operating, gradually beat in sugar and Grand Marnier, beating well between additions. Stir in ginger, cherries and chocolate; mix well.

3 Cut cake horizontally into three layers. Place one layer on serving plate; brush with syrup.

4 Spread half of the ricotta mixture over cake. Top with second layer of cake; brush with syrup. Spread with remaining ricotta mixture. Top with remaining layer of cake; brush with syrup.

5 Spread icing over top and side of cake; press nuts around side of cake. Refrigerate until ready to serve; stand at room temperature 10 minutes before serving. Cut into wedges to serve.

syrup Combine sugar, the water and Grand Marnier in small saucepan. Stir over low heat until sugar dissolves; allow to cool.

icing Place sugar and the water in small saucepan. Stir over low heat until sugar dissolves; bring to a boil. Remove from heat; cool. Beat butter until soft and creamy; gradually beat in cooled syrup, a few drops at a time. Gradually add chocolate to butter mixture; beat until well combined.

serves 8

per serving 31.3g fat; 2418kJ
tip Ricotta cake is best made a day ahead and can be refrigerated, covered, 3 days.

panettone custards with macadamia toffee

PREPARATION TIME 20 MINUTES ■ COOKING TIME 40 MINUTES (plus standing time)

500g panettone

50g softened butter

3½ cups (875ml) milk

1 vanilla bean, halved lengthways

4 eggs

1 cup (220g) sugar

¾ cup (110g) macadamias, chopped coarsely

2 tablespoons water

2 teaspoons icing sugar

1 Grease six 1-cup (250ml) ovenproof dishes.

2 Cut panettone into 1.5cm-thick rounds; spread one side of each round with butter. Cut each round into quarters; divide among prepared dishes.

3 Combine milk and vanilla bean in medium saucepan; bring almost to a boil. Remove from heat; stand, covered, 10 minutes.

4 Meanwhile, whisk eggs and half of the sugar in large heatproof jug. Gradually whisk hot milk mixture into egg mixture. Strain into large jug; discard vanilla bean.

5 Carefully pour egg mixture over panettone in prepared dishes. Place dishes in large baking dish; add enough boiling water to come halfway up sides of dishes. Bake, uncovered, in moderately slow oven about 30 minutes or until set.

6 Meanwhile, place nuts on oven tray; toast, uncovered, in oven with panettone about 10 minutes or until browned lightly. Place remaining sugar and the water in small saucepan; stir over heat, without boiling, until sugar dissolves. Boil, uncovered, without stirring, about 10 minutes or until sugar syrup is golden brown; pour over nuts. Cool; chop toffee coarsely.

7 Serve custards topped with toffee; dust tops lightly with icing sugar.

serves 6

per serving 51.5g fat; 3748kJ

tip Brioche, hot cross buns or fruit loaf can be substituted for the panettone.

croccante semi-freddo

PREPARATION TIME 20 MINUTES (plus freezing time) ■ COOKING TIME 15 MINUTES

1½ cups (240g) blanched almonds
1½ cups (330g) caster sugar
½ cup (125ml) water
4 eggs, separated
¼ cup (60ml) Amaretto
2 cups (500ml) thickened cream

1 Spread nuts in single layer on oven tray; bake, uncovered, in moderate oven about 8 minutes or until browned lightly.

2 Reserve ¼ cup of the sugar. Combine the remaining sugar with the water in medium saucepan; stir over low heat until sugar dissolves. Bring to a boil; boil, uncovered, until golden brown.

3 Add nuts to pan; stir gently until coated in toffee.

4 Pour hot toffee mixture onto lightly greased oven tray. Stand until toffee hardens. Break toffee in half. Reserve one half; place in airtight container. Process remaining toffee until chopped coarsely.

5 Beat egg yolks and reserved sugar in small bowl with electric mixer until pale and thick. Transfer mixture to large bowl; stir in liqueur. Beat cream in medium bowl with electric mixer until soft peaks form; gently fold cream into yolk mixture.

6 Beat egg whites in clean small bowl with electric mixer until soft peaks form. Gently fold half of the egg white into cream mixture; fold in chopped toffee and remaining egg white. Transfer mixture to freezer container; freeze, covered, until firm.

7 Transfer to refrigerator about 30 minutes before serving.

8 Break reserved toffee into large pieces and serve with semi-freddo.

serves 6

per serving 56.3g fat; 3459kJ
store Recipe can be made 2 days ahead and frozen, covered. Reserved toffee can be frozen for up to 3 months.

zuccotto

PREPARATION TIME 1 HOUR (plus refrigerating time) ■ COOKING TIME 5 MINUTES

20cm-round plain sponge cake
2 tablespoons brandy
2 tablespoons maraschino liqueur
90g dark chocolate
1¼ cups (310ml) cream
¼ cup (40g) icing sugar
1 cup (60g) blanched almonds, toasted, chopped coarsely
½ cup (60g) coarsely chopped roasted hazelnuts
1 teaspoon cocoa powder
1 teaspoon icing sugar, extra

1 Line 1.25-litre (5 cup) pudding bowl with a layer of damp muslin.

2 Cut cake into 1cm-thick slices. Cut each slice, diagonally, making two triangular sections.

3 Place cake around inside edge of prepared bowl, making sure narrowest end of cake is in the base of bowl; fill any gaps with pieces of cake. Trim edge; reserve any cake pieces.

4 Combine brandy and maraschino in small jug. Carefully brush cake with brandy mixture.

5 Chop a third of the chocolate finely; reserve. Melt remaining chocolate. Beat cream and sifted icing sugar in small bowl with electric mixer until firm peaks form; fold in nuts. Halve cream mixture. Fold chopped chocolate through one half; fold melted chocolate through remaining half. Spoon chopped chocolate mixture evenly over entire cake surface, leaving a cavity in centre; spoon remaining chocolate mixture into cavity.

6 Arrange reserved cake pieces over filling; brush with any remaining brandy mixture. Cover; refrigerate overnight. *[Can be made 2 days ahead to this stage.]*

7 Turn carefully onto serving plate; remove muslin. Dust top with combined cocoa and extra icing sugar.

serves 6

per serving 52.8g fat; 4087kJ
store Zuccotto is best made a day ahead and can be refrigerated, covered, 3 days.

cassata

PREPARATION TIME 1 HOUR (plus freezing time)

2 eggs, separated
½ cup (110g) icing sugar
½ cup (125ml) cream
few drops almond essence

chocolate layer

2 eggs, separated
½ cup (110g) icing sugar
½ cup (125ml) cream, beaten lightly
60g dark chocolate, melted
2 tablespoons cocoa powder
1½ tablespoons water

fruit layer

1 cup (250ml) cream
1 teaspoon vanilla essence
1 egg white, beaten lightly
⅓ cup (55g) icing sugar
2 tablespoons finely chopped red
**   glacé cherries**
2 glacé apricots (40g), chopped finely
2 glacé pineapple rings (55g),
**   chopped finely**
1 tablespoon finely chopped green
**   glacé cherries**
⅓ cup (25g) flaked almonds, toasted

1 Beat egg whites in small bowl with electric mixer until firm peaks form; gradually beat in sifted icing sugar. Fold in lightly beaten egg yolks. Beat cream and essence in small bowl with electric mixer until soft peaks form; fold into egg mixture. Pour into deep 20cm-round springform cake pan. Smooth over top; freeze, covered, until firm.

2 Spread chocolate layer over almond layer; freeze, covered, until firm.

3 Spread fruit layer over chocolate layer; freeze, covered, until firm.

4 Run small spatula around edge of cassata; wipe a hot cloth over base and side of pan. Turn cassata onto serving plate; cut into wedges to serve. Sprinkle with extra glacé cherries, if desired.

chocolate layer Beat egg whites in small bowl with electric mixer until firm peaks form; gradually beat in sifted icing sugar. Beat cream in small bowl until soft peaks form; fold in egg white mixture. Place chocolate in small bowl; stir in egg yolks. Combine cocoa and the water in small jug; stir into chocolate mixture. Fold chocolate mixture through cream mixture.

fruit layer Beat cream and essence in small bowl with electric mixer until firm peaks form. Beat egg whites in small bowl with electric mixer until firm peaks form; gradually beat in sifted icing sugar. Fold egg white mixture into cream; gently stir through fruit and nuts.

serves 8

per serving 34.6g fat; 2016kJ
store Cassata is best made a day ahead and can be frozen, covered, 3 days.

mamma's cake

PREPARATION TIME 1 HOUR (plus refrigerating time) ■ COOKING TIME 50 MINUTES (plus cooling time)

280g sponge cake mix
1 cup (250ml) strong black coffee
⅓ cup (80ml) coffee-flavoured liqueur
⅓ cup (80ml) brandy
1 tablespoon sugar

custard

½ cup (75g) cornflour
½ cup (60g) custard powder
½ cup (110g) caster sugar
2½ cups (625ml) milk
2 teaspoons vanilla essence
1½ cups (375ml) cream
30g butter
2 egg yolks, beaten lightly
90g dark chocolate, melted

1 Make up sponge mix according to directions on packet; pour mixture into greased deep 23cm-round cake pan. Bake in moderate oven 35 minutes or until cake shrinks slightly from side of pan. Turn out onto wire rack to cool. Cut cake into four even layers. Place first layer of cake on serving plate; brush well with coffee liqueur mixture.

2 Combine cold coffee, liqueur, brandy and sugar in medium bowl; mix well.

3 Spread half of the vanilla custard mixture evenly over cake. Place second layer of cake on top of custard; brush with coffee liqueur mixture. Spread a third of the chocolate custard over cake. Place third layer of cake on top of custard; brush with coffee mixture. Spread with remaining half of the vanilla custard. Top with fourth layer of cake; brush with coffee mixture.

4 Using large spatula, spread remaining chocolate custard over top and side of cake; refrigerate several hours or overnight.

custard Combine cornflour, custard powder and sugar in medium saucepan. Gradually add milk; stir until smooth and free of lumps. Add essence and cream; stir until combined. Stir over low heat until mixture boils and thickens; add butter. Simmer, uncovered, 3 minutes, stirring constantly; remove pan from heat. Add egg yolk; mix well. Place custard in large bowl. Cover with plastic food wrap; allow to become cold. Divide custard mixture in half; leave one half vanilla. Add chocolate to remaining half; mix well.

serves 8

per serving 39.5g fat; 2816kJ

tips Mamma's cake is best made a day ahead and can be refrigerated, covered, 3 days. Kahlua and Tia Maria are suitable liqueurs for this recipe.

chocolate cannoli

PREPARATION TIME 1 HOUR (plus refrigeration time) ■ COOKING TIME 25 MINUTES

1½ cups (225g) plain flour

2 tablespoons cocoa powder

2 egg yolks

1 egg, beaten lightly

2 tablespoons coffee-flavoured liqueur

1 tablespoon olive oil

1½ tablespoons water, approximately

plain flour, extra

1 egg white

vegetable oil for deep-frying

16 strawberries

ricotta filling

1kg (5 cups) ricotta cheese

½ cup (80g) icing sugar

1⅓ cups (200g) white chocolate melts, melted

⅓ cup (80ml) coffee-flavoured liqueur

chocolate sauce

⅔ cup (160ml) cream

100g dark chocolate, chopped coarsely

1 Process flour, cocoa, yolks, egg, liqueur and olive oil with enough of the water to form a soft dough; process until mixture forms a ball. Knead dough on floured surface about 5 minutes or until smooth. Wrap in plastic wrap; refrigerate 1 hour.

2 Divide dough into two portions. Roll each portion through pasta machine set on thickest setting. Fold dough in half; roll through machine, dusting with a little extra flour when necessary. Keep rolling dough through machine, adjusting setting so dough becomes thinner with each roll. Roll to second thinnest setting. Cut dough into 24 x 9cm-squares. Ensure each piece is 5mm short of the ends of the pieces of pasta or metal moulds.

3 Place whichever mould (see tip) you're using on end of each square.

4 Roll dough around mould; brush overlapping end with a little egg white. Make sure egg white does not touch the mould; press firmly to seal. Repeat with remaining squares.

5 Heat vegetable oil in large saucepan. Deep-fry cannoli, in batches, until crisp; drain on absorbent paper. Carefully remove warm cannoli shells from moulds; cool. *[Can be made a day ahead to this stage and stored in airtight container.]*

6 Spoon ricotta filling into large piping bag fitted with plain 1cm tube; pipe ricotta filling into cannoli. Serve chocolate cannoli with chocolate sauce and strawberries.

ricotta filling Beat cheese and icing sugar in large bowl with electric mixer until smooth; beat in cooled chocolate and liqueur. *[Can be made a day ahead and refrigerated, covered.]*

chocolate sauce Combine cream and chocolate in small saucepan, stir over low heat until chocolate melts.

serves 8

per serving 43.1g fat; 3129kJ

tip Cannelloni pasta shells make excellent cannoli moulds; they must be discarded after deep-frying. Metal cannoli moulds are available at specialty kitchen shops. If you use metal cannoli moulds, you're ensured of getting a sufficient number of moulds to make this recipe. You can substitute plain ready-made cannoli shells in this recipe.

zuppa inglese

PREPARATION TIME 1 HOUR (plus refrigerating time) ■ COOKING TIME 50 MINUTES (plus cooling time)

6 eggs, beaten lightly
1¼ cups (275g) caster sugar
1 cup (150g) plain flour
½ cup (75g) cornflour
1½ teaspoons baking powder
⅔ cup (160ml) milk
2 tablespoons rum
500g strawberries
200g blueberries
200g raspberries
2 teaspoons icing sugar

custard filling

½ cup (75g) cornflour
½ cup (60g) custard powder
½ cup (110g) caster sugar
2⅓ cups (580ml) milk
2 teaspoons vanilla essence
1 ⅓ cup (300ml) thickened cream
30g butter
2 egg yolks

1 Beat eggs in medium bowl with electric mixer until thick and creamy. Gradually add sugar; beat until sugar dissolves. Gently fold in flour, cornflour and baking powder. Pour mixture into greased deep 28cm-round cake pan. Bake, uncovered, in moderate oven about 35 minutes or until cake is cooked when tested; turn onto wire rack to cool. Wash and dry cake pan.

2 Split cake, horizontally, into three even layers. Place first layer of cake in clean deep 28cm-round cake pan. Brush cake with combined milk and rum. Spread half of the custard filling evenly over cake. Reserve eight strawberries for decorating top of cake; hull and slice remaining strawberries. Sprinkle half of the sliced strawberries over custard layer. Place second layer of cake on top of strawberries; brush with rum mixture. Spread remaining custard filling evenly over cake; sprinkle with remaining strawberries. Top with third layer of cake; brush with remaining rum mixture. Refrigerate, covered, several hours. *[Can be made 2 days ahead to this stage.]*

3 Turn cake onto serving plate. Decorate top of cake with reserved strawberries, blueberries and raspberries; dust top with sifted icing sugar.

custard filling Combine cornflour, custard powder and sugar in large saucepan. Gradually add milk; stir until smooth. Add essence and cream; stir until combined. Stir over low heat until custard boils and thickens; add butter. Simmer, uncovered, 3 minutes, stirring constantly; remove pan from heat. Add yolks; mix well. Transfer custard to medium heatproof bowl; cover surface with plastic wrap. Allow to become cold; beat well.

serves 12

per serving 41.1g fat; 2815kJ
store Zuppa inglese is best made a day ahead and can be refrigerated, covered, 3 days.

raspberry hazelnut cake

PREPARATION TIME 30 MINUTES ■ COOKING TIME 1 HOUR 30 MINUTES

250g butter, softened
2 cups (440g) caster sugar
6 eggs
1 cup (150g) plain flour
1/2 cup (75g) self-raising flour
1 cup (110g) hazelnut meal
2/3 cup (160g) sour cream
300g fresh or frozen raspberries

mascarpone cream
250g mascarpone cheese
1/4 cup (40g) icing sugar mixture
2 tablespoons Frangelico
1/2 cup (120g) sour cream
1/2 cup (75g) roasted hazelnuts, chopped finely

1 Position oven shelves; preheat oven to moderate. Grease deep 22cm-round cake pan; line base and side with baking paper.

2 Beat butter and sugar in medium bowl with electric mixer until light and fluffy; add eggs, one at a time, beating until just combined between additions. Mixture will curdle at this stage, but will come together later.

3 Transfer mixture to large bowl; using wooden spoon, stir in flours, hazelnut meal, sour cream and raspberries. Spread mixture into prepared pan.

4 Bake cake in moderate oven about 1 1/2 hours. Stand cake 10 minutes; turn onto wire rack. Turn top-side up to cool.

5 Place cake on serving plate. Using metal spatula, spread mascarpone cream all over cake.

mascarpone cream Combine mascarpone, icing sugar, liqueur and sour cream in medium bowl. Using wooden spoon, stir until smooth; stir in nuts.

serves 12

per serving 50.6g fat; 3012kJ
store Unfrosted cake can be kept in airtight container at room temperature 3 days, or frozen for up to 3 months; cake can be frosted a day ahead and refrigerated.
tips Don't thaw frozen raspberries, as they are less likely to 'bleed' into the cake mixture; any similar-sized berries can be substituted for the raspberries.
Any nut, such as almonds or pecans, can be substituted for the hazelnut meal; blend or process whole roasted nuts until ground finely.

sicilian cheesecake

PREPARATION TIME 30 MINUTES (plus refrigerating time)

185g plain chocolate biscuits, crushed finely

90g butter, melted

½ cup (125ml) cream

60g dark chocolate, grated coarsely

filling

625g ricotta cheese

1 cup (160g) icing sugar

1 teaspoon vanilla essence

2 tablespoons Crème de Cacao

2 tablespoons finely chopped mixed peel

60g dark chocolate, grated finely

1 Combine biscuit and butter in medium bowl; press evenly over base of 20cm-springform tin. Refrigerate while preparing filling.

2 Spoon filling over biscuit base; refrigerate at least 6 hours or overnight.

3 Just before serving, beat cream in small bowl with electric mixer until soft peaks form; spread evenly over top of cake. Sprinkle with chocolate.

filling Beat cheese, icing sugar, essence and Crème de Cacao in large bowl with electric mixer until smooth and fluffy. Add peel and chocolate; mix well.

serves 10

per serving 27.4g fat; 1816kJ

panna cotta with orange toffee sauce

PREPARATION TIME 25 MINUTES (plus standing time) ■ COOKING TIME 15 MINUTES

2¹/₂ teaspoons powdered gelatine
³/₄ cup (180ml) milk
600ml cream
²/₃ cup (150g) caster sugar
1 vanilla bean

orange toffee sauce
²/₃ cup (150g) caster sugar
¹/₄ cup (60ml) water
¹/₂ cup (125ml) orange juice

1 Lightly oil six ²/₃-cup (160ml) dishes. Sprinkle gelatine over ¹/₄ cup (60ml) of the milk. Combine remaining milk, cream and sugar in medium saucepan. Split vanilla bean; scrape out seeds. Add seeds and bean to cream mixture. Stir mixture over low heat, without boiling, until sugar dissolves; bring almost to a boil (surface of mixture should just quiver, not bubble). Remove from heat; stand, covered, 10 minutes.

2 Return cream mixture to heat until quite hot; but not boiling. Remove from heat. Stir in gelatine mixture; strain into jug. Pour cream mixture into prepared dishes; cool. Cover; refrigerate 3 hours or until set. *[Can be made 2 days ahead to this stage.]*

3 Just before serving, turn panna cotta onto serving plates; serve with orange toffee sauce. Top with sliced strawberries, if desired.

orange toffee sauce Combine sugar and the water in small heavy-based saucepan; stir over low heat, without boiling, until sugar dissolves. Brush any sugar crystals from side of pan with wet pastry brush. Boil, uncovered, without stirring, about 10 minutes or until sugar syrup is golden brown; remove from heat. Stir in juice, taking care as it will splutter fiercely. Stir over low heat, without boiling, until toffee dissolves. Cool to room temperature. *[Can be made 2 days ahead and refrigerated, covered.]*

serves 6

per serving 44.9g fat; 2627kJ
tip Serve with peaches grilled with a sprinkling of brown sugar.

soft grape gelato with nutmeg wafers

PREPARATION TIME 30 MINUTES (plus freezing time) ■ COOKING TIME 25 MINUTES (plus cooling time)

1.5kg seedless white grapes, approximately

3 egg whites

¾ cup (165g) caster sugar

nutmeg wafers

1 egg white

¼ cup (55g) caster sugar

2 tablespoons plain flour

½ teaspoon ground nutmeg

30g butter, melted

2 teaspoons cocoa powder

1 Discard grape stalks; process grapes until smooth. Push mixture through coarse strainer, pressing firmly to extract as much juice as possible. You need 3¼ cups (810ml) juice. Pour juice into large shallow cake pan. Cover with foil; freeze until just firm.

2 Beat egg whites in small bowl with electric mixer until soft peaks form. Gradually add sugar; beat until dissolved between additions.

3 Transfer frozen juice to large bowl; quickly beat with electric mixer until just smooth. Add egg white mixture; beat until combined and smooth.

4 Return mixture to pan. Cover; freeze until firm. *[Can be made 3 days ahead to this stage.]*

5 Serve grape gelato with nutmeg wafers.

nutmeg wafers Beat egg white in small bowl with electric mixer until soft peaks form. Gradually add sugar; beat until dissolved between additions. Stir in flour and nutmeg, then cooled butter; reserve 2 tablespoons of the egg mixture. Place teaspoons of egg mixture about 10cm apart on baking paper-lined oven trays, allowing four per tray; spread with spatula to about 7cm rounds. Combine reserved mixture with cocoa in small bowl; mix well. Spoon mixture into piping bag fitted with small plain tube. Pipe circles onto wafers to represent grapes. Bake, uncovered, in moderate oven about 5 minutes or until wafers are browned lightly. Lift wafers carefully from trays; place over handle of wooden spoon to give irregularly round shapes. Cool on wire racks.

serves 8

per serving 3.4g fat; 1115kJ

tips If seedless white grapes are out of season, simply purchase white grapes and seed them yourself.

The high sugar content of this dessert will ensure the gelato remains soft and will not freeze solid.

poached peaches

PREPARATION TIME 5 MINUTES (plus refrigeration time)
COOKING TIME 25 MINUTES

**1½ cups (375ml) sauternes-style
dessert wine**

2 cups (500ml) water

1 cup (220g) caster sugar

1 strip lemon rind

6 medium peaches (1kg), washed

1 Combine wine, the water, sugar and rind in
large saucepan; stir over low heat, without
boiling, until sugar dissolves. Add unpeeled
peaches; simmer, uncovered, about 20 minutes
or until tender.

2 Remove from heat; cool. Transfer syrup and
peaches to non-reactive bowl. Cover; refrigerate
3 hours. *[Can be made 2 days ahead to
this stage.]*

3 Peel peaches; discard peel and lemon rind.
Serve peaches with some of the syrup.

serves 6

per serving 0.1g fat; 1187kJ
tips Peaches can be sliced for serving.
If you choose peaches with a pink blush, poaching in their
skins will intensify the blush on the peeled fruit.

mixed berries
with mascarpone

PREPARATION TIME 10 MINUTES (plus refrigeration time)

250g strawberries, quartered

200g raspberries

200g blueberries

2 tablespoons raspberry vinegar

¼ teaspoon finely ground black pepper

½ cup (125ml) cream

200g mascarpone cheese

⅓ cup (55g) icing sugar

1 Combine berries, vinegar and pepper in large bowl.
Cover; refrigerate 1 hour or until well chilled. *[Can
be made a day ahead to this stage.]*

2 Whip cream in small bowl until soft peaks form; gently
fold in mascarpone in two batches. *[Can be made a
day ahead to this stage and refrigerated, covered.]*

3 Spoon mascarpone cream onto serving plates. Top
with berry mixture, including any juices; dust thickly
with sifted icing sugar.

serves 6

per serving 28.4g fat; 1380kJ
tip Use your favourite mixture of berries for this recipe.

honey grilled figs

PREPARATION TIME 5 MINUTES
COOKING TIME 5 MINUTES

6 large figs (480g)
2 tablespoons caster sugar
¼ cup (90g) honey
1 teaspoon vanilla essence

1 Gently break figs in half lengthways. Place figs on oven tray; sprinkle broken sides of figs with sugar.

2 Cook under hot gill about 5 minutes or until sugar melts and figs are browned lightly.

3 Meanwhile combine honey and essence in small saucepan; stir over low heat, without boiling, until honey is very runny.

4 Serve warm figs drizzled with honey mixture.

serves 6

per serving 0.2g fat; 425kJ
tips Green or purple figs are suitable for this recipe. Serve with dollops of whipped mascarpone and cream.

frozen grapes

PREPARATION TIME 10 MINUTES (plus standing and freezing)

500g green grapes
500g black grapes
¼ cup (60ml) orange-flavoured liqueur

1 Wash grapes; remove stems. Cut grapes in half; remove seeds. Combine in large bowl with liqueur. Cover; stand 1 hour.

2 Place grapes, cut-side down on baking paper lined freezer trays. Cover; freeze several hours or until firm. Transfer grapes to freezer container.

3 Serve from freezer.

serves 8

per serving 0.2g fat; 464kJ
store Recipe can be made 3 months ahead.

fruit

cakes and biscuits

If you've ever succumbed to the sweet things displayed in Italian coffee shops, you'll know just how perfect is the marriage between a cup of hot, fresh espresso and those deliciously sweet morsels. Here is a selection for you to try at home, including chocolate-coated Florentines, irresistible almond torrone and Italy's two famous festive cakes, panettone and the popular Tuscan specialty, panforte di siena (Siena cake).

white chocolate and frangelico truffles

PREPARATION TIME 35 MINUTES ■ COOKING TIME 5 MINUTES (plus refrigeration time)

¼ **cup (60ml) cream**

30g butter

250g white chocolate, chopped finely

¼ **cup (35g) roasted hazelnuts,
    chopped finely**

2 tablespoons Frangelico

200g dark chocolate, melted

100g white chocolate, melted, extra

1 Place cream, butter and white chocolate in medium saucepan; stir over low heat until chocolate melts. Stir in nuts and liqueur; pour mixture into small bowl. Cover; refrigerate, stirring occasionally, about 1 hour or until mixture thickens but does not set.

2 Roll rounded teaspoons of mixture into balls; refrigerate truffles on tray until firm.

3 Working rapidly, dip truffles in dark chocolate; roll gently in hands to coat evenly. Return truffles to tray.

4 Drizzle truffles with extra white chocolate; refrigerate, uncovered, until chocolate is completely set.

makes 32

per serving 7.3g fat; 495kJ
store Recipe best made a day ahead; store in airtight container up to a week.
tips Frangelico is a hazelnut-flavoured liqueur that marries devastatingly well with chocolate. Don't melt chocolate in a plastic bowl as plastic is not a good conductor of heat. One of the best ways to melt chocolate is in an uncovered microwave-safe container on HIGH (100%) in 30-second bursts, removing it immediately when melted.

florentines

PREPARATION TIME 40 MINUTES ■ COOKING TIME 50 MINUTES (plus cooling time)

¼ cup (35g) slivered almonds

¼ cup (30g) coarsely chopped walnuts

1 tablespoon mixed peel

1 tablespoon sultanas

5 glacé cherries (15g)

3 pieces glacé ginger (15g)

60g butter, melted

¼ cup (55g) caster sugar

1 tablespoon cream

125g dark chocolate, melted

1 Blend or process nuts, peel, sultanas, cherries and ginger until chopped finely; transfer to large bowl.

2 Stir butter and sugar in small saucepan, over low heat, until sugar dissolves; bring to a boil. Boil gently about 1 minute, or until mixture starts to turn light golden; do not stir while boiling or mixture will crystallise. Add butter mixture and cream to fruit and nut mixture; mix well.

3 Spoon heaped teaspoons of the mixture onto greased oven trays, allowing room between each for spreading. For easy handling, it is best to bake only four at a time.

4 Bake, uncovered, in moderate oven 10 minutes or until golden brown; remove from oven. Using spatula, push each florentine into round shape; allow to cool on trays 1 minute. Carefully lift each florentine from tray onto wire cooling rack; allow to cool.

5 Spoon 1 teaspoon of the chocolate onto flat side of each florentine; spread out to edge. When chocolate is almost set, run fork through chocolate to give wavy effect. Place on tray; refrigerate until chocolate is set.

makes 20

per serving 6.8g fat; 402kJ

store Recipe can be made 3 days ahead and stored in airtight container; if the weather is very humid, freeze florentines, in airtight container, for up to 1 month.

olive oil cake

PREPARATION TIME 25 MINUTES ■ COOKING TIME 45 MINUTES (plus standing time)

3 eggs, beaten lightly
1 cup (220g) caster sugar
1 tablespoon grated orange rind
2¼ cups (335g) self-raising flour
¼ cup (60ml) orange juice
½ cup (125ml) skim milk
1 cup (250ml) extra virgin olive oil
½ cup (125ml) orange juice, warmed, extra
¼ cup (40g) icing sugar

1 Oil deep 23cm-square cake pan.

2 Beat egg, sugar and rind in medium bowl with electric mixer until very thick and creamy and sugar dissolves. Stir in flour, then combined juice, milk and oil in three batches. Pour mixture into prepared pan.

3 Bake in moderately hot oven about 45 minutes or until cooked when tested. Stand cake in pan 5 minutes; turn onto wire rack placed over tray. Turn cake again so it is right-side up.

4 Pour extra juice over hot cake; sift icing sugar over top of juice. Cool before serving.

serves 10

per serving 24.8g fat; 1870kJ
tip Lemon rind and juice can be substituted for the orange.

fig and nut cake

PREPARATION TIME 25 MINUTES ■ COOKING TIME 1 HOUR (plus cooling time)

3 eggs

½ cup (110g) caster sugar

125g roasted hazelnuts, chopped coarsely

90g slivered almonds, chopped coarsely

125g dried figs, chopped coarsely

125g mixed peel, chopped coarsely

90g dark chocolate, chopped finely

1¼ cups (185g) self-raising flour

1 Beat eggs and sugar in medium bowl with electric mixer until light and fluffy. Transfer to large bowl.

2 Add nuts, fig, peel and chocolate; stir gently until combined.

3 Gently fold sifted flour into mixture. Place mixture into greased 15cm x 25cm loaf pan; bake in moderate oven about 1 hour or until light golden brown and cooked when tested. Allow to cool slightly in pan; turn onto wire rack to cool completely before cutting.

serves 8

per serving 21.7g fat; 1896kJ

tip Fig and nut cake is best made a day ahead. Can be stored in airtight container, 3 days.

almond crunch

PREPARATION TIME 15 MINUTES ■ COOKING TIME 50 MINUTES (plus cooling time)

1³/4 cups (385g) caster sugar

2 tablespoons lemon juice

**1 cup (160g) whole
  blanched almonds**

¹/4 cup (90g) golden syrup

1¹/4 cups (300ml) cream

1 Combine ¹/2 cup of the sugar and juice in medium saucepan; stir over low heat, without boiling, until sugar dissolves. Bring to a boil, without stirring, about 6 minutes or until sugar turns dark golden brown. Remove pan from heat. Add almonds; mix well. Drop mixture onto marble slab or oven tray that has been sprinkled with water; cool.

2 Place remaining sugar, golden syrup and cream in large heavy-based saucepan; bring to a boil over moderate heat, stirring. Reduce heat; continue cooking, without stirring, until a little dropped into cold water forms a ball between two fingers (126°C on a sugar (candy) thermometer). This will take about 30 minutes; be careful the mixture does not boil over.

3 Blend or process almond toffee mixture, in batches, until fairly fine.

4 Mix blended toffee into the hot mixture. Pour into well-oiled 19cm x 29cm rectangular slice pan; cool. Mark out into pieces about 2.5cm square; cut into squares when cold.

makes 75

per serving 2.3g fat; 172kJ

store Almond crunch can be made 3 days ahead and stored in airtight container in a cool, dry place.

panettone

PREPARATION TIME 40 MINUTES (plus standing time) ■ COOKING TIME 45 MINUTES

½ cup (85g) raisins
¼ cup (40g) mixed peel
½ cup (80g) sultanas
⅓ cup (80ml) sweet marsala
2 tablespoons dry yeast
1 teaspoon caster sugar
¼ cup (60ml) warm milk
5 cups (750g) plain flour
1 teaspoon salt
¼ cup (55g) caster sugar, extra
3 eggs, beaten lightly
3 egg yolks
2 teaspoons grated orange rind
1 teaspoon vanilla essence
100g butter, softened
1 cup (250ml) warm milk, extra
1 egg, beaten lightly, extra

1 Grease two deep 20cm-round cake pans. Using string, tie a collar of greased foil around outside of prepared pans, bringing foil about 6cm above edges of pans.

2 Combine fruit with marsala in small bowl. Cover; stand 30 minutes. Combine yeast, sugar and milk in small bowl; whisk until yeast dissolves. Cover bowl; stand in warm place about 10 minutes or until mixture is frothy.

3 Place flour, salt and extra sugar in large bowl; make well in centre. Add eggs and egg yolks, then rind, essence, butter, extra milk, yeast mixture and undrained fruit mixture.

4 Using wooden spoon, beat dough vigorously about 5 minutes (this beating is important). The dough will be soft like cake batter, and will become elastic and leave the side of the bowl. Cover bowl with greased plastic wrap; stand in warm place about 30 minutes or until dough doubles in size. Turn dough onto floured surface; knead about 10 minutes or until smooth. Cut dough in half; knead each half on well-floured surface about 5 minutes or until dough loses its stickiness. Press dough into prepared pans. Cover; stand in warm place about 30 minutes or until dough doubles in size. Brush with extra egg. Bake, uncovered, in moderately hot oven about 15 minutes. Reduce heat to moderate; bake, uncovered, further 30 minutes. Cool on wire racks.

makes 2

per loaf 71.7g fat; 10881kJ
store Recipe can be made 2 days ahead and stored in airtight container.

sicilian creams

PREPARATION TIME 35 MINUTES ■ COOKING TIME 20 MINUTES (plus cooling time)

1³/4 cups (260g) self-raising flour

60g butter

¹/2 cup (110g) caster sugar

1 teaspoon grated lemon rind

1 teaspoon vanilla essence

1 egg

¹/4 cup (60ml) milk

¹/4 cup (60ml) cream

2 tablespoons icing sugar

1 tablespoon water

1 tablespoon liqueur

1 tablespoon icing sugar, extra

1 Place flour in large bowl; rub in butter. Add sugar; mix well. Make well in centre of mixture; add combined rind, vanilla, egg and milk. Using wooden spoon, mix to a soft, pliable dough.

2 Turn dough onto lightly floured surface; knead gently until smooth. Dough should be soft and pliable.

3 Roll dough out gently until 1cm thick. Cut into rounds using 5cm cutter; place on lightly greased oven trays, about 2.5cm apart. Bake, uncovered, in moderate oven about 15 minutes or until light golden brown; cool on wire rack. *[Can be made 2 days ahead to this stage and refrigerated, covered.]*

4 Beat cream and icing sugar in small bowl with electric mixer until firm peaks form. Using fine serrated knife, split each biscuit in half, horizontally; brush cut side of each top half of biscuit with combined water and liqueur. Join biscuits with cream; dust with extra icing sugar.

makes 12

per serving 7.9g fat; 833kJ

tip Sicilian creams are best assembled close to serving. Any liqueur can be used to flavour these biscuits, e.g. Galliano, Grand Marnier, Cointreau or Amaretto.

amaretti

PREPARATION TIME 15 MINUTES (plus standing time) ■ COOKING TIME 15 MINUTES

1 cup (125g) almond meal
1 cup (220g) caster sugar
2 large egg whites
½ teaspoon vanilla essence
2 drops almond essence
20 blanched almonds

1 Beat almond meal, sugar, egg whites and essences in medium bowl with electric mixer, on medium speed, 3 minutes; stand 5 minutes.

2 Spoon mixture into piping bag fitted with 1cm plain tube; pipe in circular motion from centre, to make biscuits about 4cm in diameter leaving 2cm between each. Top with almonds.

3 Bake, uncovered, in moderate oven, about 12 minutes or until tops are browned lightly. Stand on trays 5 minutes before removing with metal spatula. Cool on wire rack.

makes 20

per serving 4.1g fat; 366kJ
store Amaretti can be made 3 days ahead and stored in airtight container.

almond torrone

PREPARATION TIME 15 MINUTES (plus standing time) ■ COOKING TIME 20 MINUTES

A sugar (candy) thermometer, available from kitchenware stores, is essential for this recipe.
Place thermometer in large saucepan of simmering water while syrup is starting to heat.
This will stop thermometer cracking when placed in syrup. Once syrup is correct
temperature, return thermometer to pan of water; remove from heat. When cool, rinse and
dry. You will also need a powerful electric mixer. Choose one on a stand as they generally
have more powerful motors than most hand-held electric mixers.

2 sheets (15cm x 20cm) rice paper
3 cups (480g) blanched almonds
1/2 cup (175g) honey
1 1/3 cups (300g) caster sugar
2 tablespoons water
1 egg white

1 Preheat oven to moderate (180°C). Lightly grease 8cm x 26cm bar pan.
   Line pan with a strip of baking paper, covering base and extending
   5cm over two long sides. Place one sheet of rice paper in pan,
   covering base and extending up two long sides.

2 Spread almonds in single layer on oven tray; bake in moderate oven
   about 10 minutes or until well browned. Transfer to large heatproof
   bowl. Meanwhile, combine honey, sugar and the water in small
   saucepan; stir over low heat, without boiling, until sugar dissolves.
   Using pastry brush dipped in hot water, brush down side of pan to
   dissolve all sugar crystals.

3 Bring syrup to a boil; boil, uncovered, without stirring, about 10 minutes
   or until syrup reaches 164°C on sugar thermometer. Remove
   immediately from heat. Just before syrup is ready, beat egg white in
   small heatproof bowl with electric mixer until soft peaks form. With
   motor operating, add hot syrup to egg white in a thin stream. Beat until
   all syrup is added.

4 Working quickly, transfer egg white mixture to bowl with almonds; stir
   until combined. Spoon mixture into prepared pan; press in firmly. Cut
   remaining sheet of rice paper to fit top of nougat; press on lightly. Stand
   about 2 hours or until cooled to room temperature. When cooled,
   transfer to airtight container; do not refrigerate. Cut into 1cm slices.

makes 25 slices

per slice 10.6g fat; 764.2kJ
store Torrone can be made a week ahead and stored in airtight container in a cool,
dry place.
tip This type of rice paper, generally imported from Holland, is whiter than the Asian
variety and looks more like a grainy sheet of paper.

siena cake

PREPARATION TIME 30 MINUTES ■ COOKING TIME 1 HOUR (plus cooling time)

¾ **cup (120g) blanched almonds, toasted, chopped coarsely**

1 **cup (125g) coarsely chopped roasted hazelnuts**

¼ **cup (60g) finely chopped glacé apricots**

¼ **cup (55g) finely chopped glacé pineapple**

⅓ **cup (55g) mixed peel, chopped finely**

⅔ **cup (100g) plain flour**

2 **tablespoons cocoa powder**

1 **teaspoon ground cinnamon**

⅓ **cup (75g) caster sugar**

½ **cup (175g) honey**

60g **dark chocolate, melted**

1   Combine nuts, apricots, pineapple, peel, flour, cocoa and cinnamon in large bowl; mix well.

2   Lightly grease 20cm-round sandwich pan. Line base and side with baking paper.

3   Place sugar and honey in medium saucepan; stir over low heat until sugar dissolves, brushing down side of pan to dissolve any sugar crystals. Bring to a boil; reduce heat. Simmer, uncovered, about 5 minutes or until syrup forms a soft ball when a few drops are dropped into a glass of cold water. Add syrup and chocolate to fruit and nut mixture; mix well.

4   Spread mixture quickly and evenly into prepared pan. Bake, uncovered, in moderately slow oven 35 minutes; cool in pan. Turn out; remove paper. Wrap in foil; leave at least one day before cutting.

serves 8

per serving   21.1g fat; 1925kJ

store   Recipe can be made 3 weeks ahead and wrapped tightly in foil.

tip   Siena cake is a perfect accompaniment for after-dinner coffee. Cut into thin wedges or slices about 1cm thick, then into small pieces.

espresso syrup cake

PREPARATION TIME 20 MINUTES ■ COOKING TIME 45 MINUTES

3 teaspoons instant espresso-style coffee

1 tablespoon hot water

3 eggs, beaten lightly

3/4 cup (165g) caster sugar

1 cup (150g) self-raising flour

1 tablespoon cocoa powder

150g butter, melted

espresso syrup

3/4 cup (165g) caster sugar

3/4 cup (180ml) water

3 teaspoons instant espresso-style coffee

1 Grease 21cm baba pan. Combine coffee and the water in small jug; stir until dissolved.

2 Beat egg in small bowl with electric mixer about 8 minutes or until thick and creamy; gradually add sugar, beating until dissolved between additions. Fold in sifted flour and cocoa, then butter and coffee mixture; pour mixture into prepared pan.

3 Bake, uncovered, in moderate oven about 40 minutes. Stand cake in pan 5 minutes; turn onto wire rack over tray. Reserve 1/4 cup (60ml) espresso syrup; drizzle remaining hot syrup over hot cake. Serve with reserved syrup.

espresso syrup Combine ingredients in small saucepan; stir over heat, without boiling, until sugar dissolves. Bring to a boil; transfer to heatproof jug.

serves 8

per serving 17.7g fat; 1627kJ

store Recipe can be made 3 days ahead and stored in airtight container.

lemon and pistachio biscotti

PREPARATION TIME 20 MINUTES (plus refrigeration time)
COOKING TIME 40 MINUTES (plus cooling time)

60g butter, chopped coarsely
1 cup (220g) caster sugar
1 teaspoon vanilla essence
1 tablespoon lemon rind
4 eggs
2¼ cups (335g) plain flour
1 teaspoon baking powder
½ teaspoon bicarbonate of soda
1 cup (150g) shelled pistachios, chopped coarsely
2 tablespoons caster sugar, extra

1 Beat butter, sugar, essence and rind in medium bowl until just combined. Add three of the eggs, one at a time, beating until combined between additions. Stir in flour, baking powder, soda and nuts. Cover; refrigerate 1 hour.

2 Knead dough on lightly floured surface until smooth but still sticky. Halve dough; shape each half into a 30cm log. Place each log on greased oven tray. Combine remaining egg with 1 tablespoon water in small bowl. Brush egg mixture over logs; sprinkle thickly with extra sugar.

3 Bake, uncovered, in moderate oven about 20 minutes or until firm; cool on trays.

4 Using serrated knife, cut logs, diagonally, into 1cm slices. Place slices on ungreased oven trays.

5 Bake, uncovered, in moderately slow oven about 15 minutes or until dry and crisp, turning halfway through cooking; cool on wire racks.

makes 60

per biscotti 2.5g fat; 262kJ
store Biscotti can be stored in airtight container 2 weeks.

aniseed biscotti

PREPARATION TIME 40 MINUTES (plus refrigeration time)
COOKING TIME 1 HOUR (plus cooling time)

125g unsalted butter
¾ cup (165g) caster sugar
3 eggs
2 tablespoons brandy
1 tablespoon grated lemon rind
1½ cups (225g) plain flour
¾ cup (110g) self-raising flour
½ teaspoon salt
125g blanched almonds, toasted, chopped coarsely
1 tablespoon ground aniseed

1 Cream butter and sugar in large bowl; add eggs, one at a time, beating well after each addition. Add brandy and rind; mix well. Stir flours and salt into butter mixture.

2 Stir nuts and aniseed into dough; refrigerate, covered, 1 hour.

3 Halve dough; shape each half into a 30cm log. Place on greased oven tray.

4 Bake, uncovered, in moderate oven 20 minutes or until lightly golden brown; cool on trays.

5 Using serrated knife, cut logs diagonally into 1cm slices. Place slices on ungreased oven trays.

6 Bake, uncovered, in moderate oven about 25 minutes or until dry and crisp, turning halfway through cooking; cool on wire racks.

makes 40

per serving 4.9g fat; 397kJ
store Biscotti can be stored in airtight container 2 weeks.

swirled choc-almond biscotti

PREPARATION TIME 25 MINUTES (plus refrigeration time)
COOKING TIME 45 MINUTES (plus cooling time)

60g butter
1 cup (220g) caster sugar
1 teaspoon vanilla essence
3 eggs
2¼ cups (335g) plain flour
1 teaspoon baking powder
½ teaspoon bicarbonate of soda
1½ cups (240g) almond kernels, chopped coarsely
¼ cup (25g) cocoa powder
¼ cup (35g) plain flour, extra

1 Beat butter, sugar and essence in medium bowl until just combined. Add eggs, one at a time, beating until combined between additions. Stir in flour, baking powder, soda and nuts. Cover; refrigerate 1 hour.

2 Halve dough. Knead cocoa into one half of dough; shape into a 30cm log. Knead extra flour into remaining dough; shape into a 30cm log. Gently twist cocoa log and plain log together; place on greased oven tray. Bake, uncovered, in moderate oven about 45 minutes or until firm; cool on tray.

3 Using serrated knife cut log, diagonally, into 1cm slices. Place slices on ungreased oven trays.

4 Bake, uncovered, in moderately slow oven about 15 minutes or until dry and crisp, turning halfway through cooking; cool on wire racks.

makes 25

per biscotti 8.2g fat; 715kJ
store Biscotti can be stored in airtight container 2 weeks.

coffee and hazelnut biscotti

PREPARATION TIME 35 MINUTES (plus setting time)
COOKING TIME 40 MINUTES (plus cooling time)

½ cup (110g) caster sugar
1 egg, beaten lightly
¾ cup (110g) plain flour
½ teaspoon baking powder
1 tablespoon espresso-style instant coffee
1 cup (150g) hazelnuts, toasted, chopped coarsely
100g dark chocolate, melted

1 Whisk sugar and egg together in medium bowl; stir in flour, baking powder and coffee. Stir in nuts; mix to a sticky dough. Using floured hands, roll into a 20cm log. Place on greased oven tray.

2 Bake, uncovered, in moderate oven about 25 minutes or until browned lightly and firm; cool on tray.

3 Using a serrated knife, cut log, diagonally, into 1cm slices. Place slices on ungreased oven tray.

4 Bake, uncovered, in moderately slow oven about 15 minutes or until dry and crisp, turning halfway through cooking; cool on wire racks.

5 Spread chocolate over one cut side of each biscotti. Allow to set at room temperature.

makes 20

per biscotti 6.5g fat; 486kJ
store Biscotti can be stored in airtight container 2 weeks.

biscotti

glossary

almond
essence almond extract.
kernels shelled almonds; brown skin is intact.
meal finely ground almonds; powdered to a flour-like texture. Used in baking or as a thickening agent.

almonds
blanched skins removed.
flaked paper-thin slices.
slivered small lengthways-cut pieces.

Amaretto an almond-flavoured liqueur.

anchovy fillets salted fillets; available rolled or flat and packaged or canned in oil.

aniseed, ground ground leaf of the aniseed myrtle plant.

artichoke
globe large flower-bud of a member of the thistle family; having tough petal-like leaves, edible in part when cooked.

hearts tender centre of the globe artichoke; sold in cans or loose, in brine.

bacon rashers slices of bacon; made from pork side, cured and smoked.

baking powder a raising agent consisting mainly of 2 parts cream of tartar to 1 part bicarbonate of soda (baking soda).

balmain bugs a type of sand lobster also known as shovelnose lobster or Moreton Bay bug; they taste like lobster, but the flesh is easier to remove from shell. Substitute lobster if unavailable.

basil an aromatic member of the mint family with both culinary and medicinal uses. There are many varieties, however, the most commonly used is sweet basil.

bay leaves aromatic leaves from the bay tree; use fresh or dried.

beans

borlotti also known as roman beans; pale pink with dark red spots, eat fresh or dried.
broad also known as fava beans; available fresh, canned and frozen. Fresh beans are best peeled twice; discard both the outer long green pod and the sandy-green tough inner shell.

dried cannellini small, dried white bean similar in appearance and flavour to great northern and navy or haricot beans.

dried haricot small, dried white bean similar in appearance and flavour to other *Phaseolus vulgaris*, great northern, navy and cannelloni beans.

beef
eye-fillet tenderloin.
minced also known as ground beef.
rump steak boneless tender cut.
sirloin steaks good-quality steak with T-bone or boneless; New York-style steak.

bicarbonate of soda also known as baking soda.

blue-eye
cutlets thick, crossways-slices of fish, cut through skin and bones.
fillets tender flesh, cut lengthways.

blue swimmer crabs also known as sand crabs; Atlantic blue crabs.

brandy spirit distilled from wine.

breadcrumbs
packaged fine-textured, crunchy, purchased, white breadcrumbs; will keep almost indefinitely, in an airtight container.
stale also known as soft breadcrumbs; 1- or 2-day old bread made into crumbs by grating, blending or processing. Can be frozen for up to 6 months.

butter use salted or unsalted ('sweet') butter; 125g is equal to 1 stick butter.

buttermilk low-fat milk cultured to give a slightly sour, tangy taste; low-fat yogurt can be substituted.

calamari a type of mollusc; also known as squid. Slice hood thinly to form rings.

calves liver available from butchers; remove silvery membrane after rinsing.

capers

baby capers

capers grey-green buds of a warm climate (usually Mediterranean) shrub, sold either dried and salted or pickled in a vinegar brine. The smaller capers are better.

capsicum also known as pepper, or bell pepper; available in red, yellow and green varieties. Seeds and membranes should be discarded before use.

cardamom available in pod, seed or ground form with a distinctive aromatic, sweetly rich flavour. Native to India, it's one of the world's most expensive spices.

cashews we used unsalted roasted cashews in this book.

chicken
breast fillets breast halved, skinned and boned.

drumsticks leg with skin intact.
mince finely ground fresh chicken.
tenderloins thin strip of meat lying just under the breast; especially good for stir-fry cooking.
thigh cutlets thigh with skin and centre bone intact; also known as a chicken chop.

chilli
dried, flakes crushed dried chillies.
powder made from ground chillies; the Asian variety is the hottest. It can be used as a substitute for fresh chillies in the proportion of 1/2 teaspoon ground chilli powder to 1 medium chopped fresh chilli.
thai small, medium hot and bright-red to dark-green in colour.

flat-leaf parsley
chives
mint
y sley
basil
coriander
oregano

chives related to the onion and leek, with a subtle onion flavour.
garlic have flat leaves and a stronger flavour than chives.

chocolate
bits also known as chocolate chips; available in milk, white and dark varieties. Made of cocoa liquor, cocoa butter, sugar and an emulsifier, these hold their shape in baking and are ideal for decorating.
dark eating chocolate; made of cocoa liquor, cocoa butter and sugar.
drinking powder sweetened cocoa powder.

chocolate-flavoured liqueur Crème de Cacao.

cinnamon sticks dried inner bark of the shoots of the cinnamon tree. Also available in ground form.

clams we used a small ridge-shelled variety of this bivalve mollusc; also known as vongole.

cloves dried flower buds of a tropical tree; can be used whole or in ground form.

cocoa powder ground cocoa beans with half of the butter removed.

coffee-flavoured liqueur Tia Maria, Kahlua.

cooking-oil spray vegetable oil in an aerosol can; available in supermarkets.

coriander also known as cilantro or chinese parsley; bright-green-leafed herb with a pungent flavour.
seeds Grind seeds after briefly dry-roasting to maintain vibrancy; do not substitute for fresh coriander.

cornflour also known as cornstarch; used as a thickening agent in cooking.

cream we used fresh cream in this book, unless otherwise stated. Also known as pure cream and pouring cream; has no additives unlike commercially thickened cream. Minimum fat content 35%.
sour a thick commercially-cultured soured cream good for dips, toppings and baked cheesecakes. Minimum fat content 35%.
thickened a whipping cream containing a thickener. Minimum fat content 35%.

curly endive also known as frisee; a curly-leafed green vegetable, mainly used in salads.

custard powder powdered thickening agent used in custard; contains starch.

dark rum we prefer to use an underproof (not overproof) for a more subtle flavour.

dill tiny green-yellow flowers with light green, feathery leaves.

dry yeast a leavening agent used in breads.

dry mustard available in powder form.

duck we used whole ducks; available from most specialty chicken shops.

eggplant also known as aubergine. Depending on age, they may require slicing and salting to reduce bitterness; rinse and dry well before using. Also baby eggplant.

fennel also known as finocchio or anise; can be eaten raw in salads or braised or fried as a vegetable accompaniment.

flour
white plain an all-purpose wheat flour.
self raising plain flour sifted with baking powder in the proportion of 1 cup flour to 2 teaspoons baking powder.

Frangelico hazelnut-flavoured liqueur.

Galliano clear yellow-coloured Italian liqueur made from an infusion of various herbs and flowers.

garfish slender, silvery fish with a fine, sweet flavour; usually sold whole.

garlic a bulb contains many cloves which can be crushed, sliced, chopped, or used whole, peeled or unpeeled.

gelatine also known as gelatin; we used powdered gelatine. It is also available in sheet form known as leaf gelatine.

ginger also known as green or root ginger; the thick gnarled root of a tropical plant.

glacé fruit fruit preserved in sugar syrup.

golden syrup a by-product of refined sugarcane; pure maple syrup or honey can be substituted.

Grand Marnier orange-flavoured liqueur based on Cognac-brandy.

green ginger wine alcoholic sweet wine with the taste of fresh ginger; dry (white) vermouth or syrup from a jar of preserved ginger can be substituted.

ham
leg good quality ham carved off the bone.
shaved very thinly sliced ham.

hazelnuts also known as filberts. Plump, grape-sized, rich, sweet nut having a brown skin (removed by rubbing heated nuts together in a tea-towel).

herbs we used dried (not ground) herbs in the ratio of 1 teaspoon dried herbs to 4 teaspoons chopped fresh herbs.

lebanese cucumber also known as european or burpless cucumber; this variety is long, slender and thin-skinned.

leek a member of the onion family; resembles the green onion but is much larger.

lemon thyme a variety of thyme with a lemony fragrance.

lettuce
oak leaf also known as Feville de Chene. Available in red and green leaf varieties.
butter a round, dark green lettuce with soft leaves.

cos also known as Roma; has crisp elongated leaves.

iceberg a heavy, firm, round lettuce with tightly packed leaves and crisp texture.

radicchio a type of Italian lettuce with dark burgundy leaves.

rocket also known as arugula, rugla and rucola; a peppery-tasting green leaf which can be eaten raw in salads or cooked in soups, risottos and the like.

macadamias native to Australia; a rich and buttery nut. Store in refrigerator because of high oil content.

maple-flavoured syrup also known as golden or pancake syrup; made from cane sugar and artificial maple flavouring. It is not a substitute for pure maple syrup.

maraschino liqueur a cherry-flavoured liqueur.

marsala a sweet fortified wine originally from Sicily.

mayonnaise a paste consisting of oil, egg and vinegar.

milk we used full-cream homogenised milk unless otherwise specified.

evaporated unsweetened canned milk from which water has been extracted by evaporation.

skim we used milk with 0.1% fat content.

mint a tangy, aromatic herb available fresh or dried.

mixed peel candied citrus peel.

mixed spice a blend of ground spices usually consisting of cinnamon, allspice and nutmeg.

mizuna a Japanese green salad leaf with a delicate mustard flavour; used in mesclun.

mushrooms

button small, cultivated white mushrooms having a delicate, subtle flavour.

flat large, soft, flat mushrooms with a rich earthy flavour; sometimes misnamed field mushrooms.

swiss brown light to dark brown mushrooms with full-bodied flavour. Button or cup mushrooms can be substituted.

mussels purchase from a reliable fish market. Mussels must be tightly closed when bought, indicating they are alive. Before cooking, scrub shells with a strong brush and remove 'beards'. Discard any shells that do not open after cooking.

mustard

dijon a pale brown, distinctively flavoured, fairly mild French mustard.

seeded French-style mustard with crushed seeds.

nutmeg the dried nut of an evergreen tree native to Indonesia; available in ground form or you can grate your own with a fine grater.

octopus, baby must be tenderised before being cooked; curled up tentacles are an indication of tenderness.

olive oil mono-unsaturated; made from the pressing of tree-ripened olives. Extra light or light describes the mild flavour, not the fat levels. Extra virgin and virgin are the highest quality olive oils, obtained from the first pressings of the olive.

olives

kalamata a dark olive, preserved in salt and oil; Greek in origin.

small stuffed green olives stuffed with pimento.

onion

red also known as spanish, red spanish or bermuda onion; a sweet-flavoured, large, purple-red onion.

green also known as scallion or (incorrectly) shallot; an immature onion picked before the bulb has formed, having a long, bright-green edible stalk.

orange-flavoured liqueur Grand Marnier.

oregano a member of the mint family; related to but spicier than marjoram.

panettone an Italian cake, containing dried fruit and nuts.

parsley

curly most familiar variety with bright-green, tightly curled leaves.

flat-leaf also known as continental parsley or italian parsley.

passionfruit also known as granadilla; a small tropical fruit, native to Brazil, comprised of a tough outer skin encasing edible black sweet-sour seeds.

pear, corella miniature dessert pear with colourful green skin and a gold and red blush; juicy and delicious, it is popular in cheese platters.

peppercorns available in black, white, red or green; we used the black dried variety.

pesto made from garlic, oil, vinegar, pine nuts, basil, herbs and spices. Available bottled from supermarkets.

pine nuts also known as pignoli; small, cream-coloured kernels obtained from the cones of different varieties of pine trees.

pistachios pale green, delicately flavoured nut inside hard off-white shells. To peel, soak shelled nuts in boiling water about 5 minutes; drain, then pat dry with absorbent paper.

pitta also known as lebanese bread or pita; a wheat-flour pocket bread sold in large, flat pieces separating into two thin rounds.

pizza bases commercially packaged, pre-cooked, wheat-flour round bases.

pork

butterfly steaks skinless, boneless mid-loin chop, split in half and flattened.

rack row of cutlets.

potato, desiree long, oval potato; smooth pink skin with yellow flesh. Most suitable for salads, roasting, boiling and mashing; not suitable for frying.

prawns also known as shrimp.

pumpkin also known as squash; we used butternut pumpkin.

puy lentils a very fine, dark blue-green, fast cooking lentil originally from Le Puy in France.

quail a small, delicate flavoured, domestically grown game bird, ranging in weight from 250g to 300g.

rabbit wild rabbit is gamy in flavour with dark coloured flesh; farmed rabbit has a more subtle flavour and is paler in colour.

white medium-grain   *brown long-grain*

white long-grain   *arborio*

rice

arborio small, round-grain rice well-suited to absorb a large amount of liquid; especially suitable for risottos.

brown natural whole grain.

long-grain elongated grain, remains separate when cooked; most popular steaming rice in Asia.

white is hulled and polished; can be short- or long-grained.

rice paper contrary to popular belief, this type of rice paper is made from the pith of a small Asian tree, not rice. The fine, glossy paper is edible and very useful when making biscuits and confectionery.

rolled oats also known as oatmeal or porridge; oat grouts, husked, steamed-softened, flattened with rollers, dried and packaged as a cereal product.

saffron stigma of a member of the crocus family; available in strands or ground form. Imparts a yellow-orange colour to food once infused. The most expensive spice in the world; keep refrigerated.

italian

milano

salami
italian made from pork and red capsicum; it is not spicy.
milano made from pork, garlic, white wine and peppercorns; quite spicy.

salmon red-pink firm-flesh fish with few bones; it has a moist delicate flavour.

sardines small silvery fish with soft, oily flesh.

savoy cabbage large, heavy head with crinkled dark-green outer leaves; a fairly mild tasting cabbage.

scallop a bivalve mollusc with fluted shell valve; we used scallops with the coral (roe) attached.

seafood marinara mix a mixture of uncooked, chopped seafood available from fish markets and fishmongers.

semolina made from durum wheat; milled, various textured granules, all of these finer than flour. The main ingredient in good pastas and some kinds of gnocchi.

sesame seeds black and white are the most common of the tiny oval seeds harvested from the tropical plant *Sesamum indicum*; a good source of calcium.

silverbeet also known as swiss chard and mistakenly, spinach; a member of the beet family with tasty green leaves and celery-like stem.

smoked haddock white flesh with a milky smoky flavour and an orange skin.

smoked salmon soft, slightly moist flesh with a delicate flavour.

snow peas also called mange tout ('eat all'). Snow pea tendrils, the growing shoots of the plant, are sold by greengrocers.

spinach correct name for english spinach; the green vegetable often called spinach is correctly known as silverbeet. Delicate, crinkled green leaves on thin stems; high in iron. Also, baby spinach.

sponge finger biscuits, packet also known as savoiardi, savoy biscuits or ladyfingers; Italian-style, crisp biscuits made from a sponge-cake mixture.

squash also known as patty-pan, scallopine or summer squash; small, flattish yellow or green-skinned squash.

stock 1 cup (250ml) stock is the equivalent of 1 cup (250ml) water plus 1 crumbled stock cube (or 1 teaspoon stock powder).

sugar we used coarse, granulated table sugar, also known as crystal sugar, unless otherwise specified.
brown an extremely soft, fine granulated sugar retaining molasses for its characteristic colour and flavour.
caster also known as superfine or finely granulated table sugar.
icing also known as confectioners' sugar or powdered sugar. We used icing sugar mixture, not pure icing sugar, unless specified.

sugar snap peas small pods with tiny, formed peas inside; they are eaten whole, cooked or uncooked.

swordfish steaks an oily firm-fleshed fish.

thyme leaves have a warm, herby taste; can be used fresh or dried.

tomato
pasta sauce bottled prepared sauce available from supermarkets.
paste triple-concentrated tomato puree used to flavour soups, stews, sauces and casseroles.
puree canned pureed tomatoes (not tomato paste). Substitute fresh peeled and pureed tomatoes.

tomatoes
canned whole peeled tomatoes in natural juices.
cherry also known as tiny tim or tom thumb tomatoes; small and round.
egg also known as plum or roma, these are smallish, oval-shaped tomatoes much used in Italian cooking or salads.
sun-dried we used those bottled in oil, unless otherwise specified.

turmeric, ground a member of the ginger family, its root is dried and ground, giving a rich yellow powder. It is intensely pungent in taste but not hot.

vanilla
bean dried long, thin pod from a tropical golden orchid; the minuscule black seeds inside the bean impart a luscious vanilla flavour in cooking.
essence we used imitation vanilla essence.

veal
boned rolled leg of veal.
nut a lean cut from the leg.
schnitzels thinly sliced steak.
shin also known as osso buco.
steaks schnitzel.

vegetable oil any number of oils sourced from plants rather than animal fats.

vinegar
balsamic a matured Italian vinegar; use sparingly.
raspberry made from fresh raspberries steeped in a white wine vinegar.
red wine based on fermented red wine.
sherry natural vinegar aged in oak, as per the traditional Spanish system.
white made from spirit of cane sugar.
white wine made from white wine.

white fish fillets any non-oily fish; bream, flathead, whiting, snapper, jewfish and ling. Redfish also comes into this category.

whitebait small, silver-coloured fish eaten whole; no gutting is required. Rinse thoroughly and drain well before using.

witlof also known as chicory or belgian endive.

zucchini also known as courgette; green yellow or grey members of the squash family having edible flowers.

index

facts and figures

Wherever you live, you'll be able to use our recipes with the help of these easy-to-follow conversions. While these conversions are approximate only, the difference between an exact and the approximate conversion of various liquid and dry measures is but minimal and will not affect your cooking results.

dry measures

metric	imperial
15g	1/2oz
30g	1oz
60g	2oz
90g	3oz
125g	4oz (1/4lb)
155g	5oz
185g	6oz
220g	7oz
250g	8oz (1/2lb)
280g	9oz
315g	10oz
345g	11oz
375g	12oz (3/4lb)
410g	13oz
440g	14oz
470g	15oz
500g	16oz (1lb)
750g	24oz (1 1/2lb)
1kg	32oz (2lb)

liquid measures

metric	imperial
30ml	1 fluid oz
60ml	2 fluid oz
100ml	3 fluid oz
125ml	4 fluid oz
150ml	5 fluid oz (1/4 pint/1 gill)
190ml	6 fluid oz
250ml	8 fluid oz
300ml	10 fluid oz (1/2 pint)
500ml	16 fluid oz
600ml	20 fluid oz (1 pint)
1000ml (1 litre)	1 3/4 pints

helpful measures

metric	imperial
3mm	1/8in
6mm	1/4in
1cm	1/2in
2cm	3/4in
2.5cm	1in
5cm	2in
6cm	2 1/2in
8cm	3in
10cm	4in
13cm	5in
15cm	6in
18cm	7in
20cm	8in
23cm	9in
25cm	10in
28cm	11in
30cm	12in (1ft)

helpful measures

The difference between one country's measuring cups and another's is, at most, within a 2 or 3 teaspoon variance. (For the record, 1 Australian metric measuring cup holds approximately 250ml.) The most accurate way of measuring dry ingredients is to weigh them. When measuring liquids, use a clear glass or plastic jug with the metric markings. (One Australian metric tablespoon holds 20ml; one Australian metric teaspoon holds 5ml.)

Note: North America, NZ and the UK use 15ml tablespoons. All cup and spoon measurements are level.

We use large eggs having an average weight of 60g.

how to measure

When using graduated metric measuring cups, shake dry ingredients loosely into the appropriate cup. Do not tap the cup on a bench or tightly pack the ingredients unless directed to do so. Level top of measuring cups and measuring spoons with a knife. When measuring liquids, place a clear glass or plastic jug with metric markings on a flat surface to check accuracy at eye level.

oven temperatures

These oven temperatures are only a guide. Always check the manufacturer's manual.

	°C (Celsius)	°F (Fahrenheit)	Gas Mark
Very slow	120	250	1
Slow	150	300	2
Moderately slow	160	325	3
Moderate	180 - 190	350 - 375	4
Moderately hot	200 - 210	400 - 425	5
Hot	220 - 230	450 - 475	6
Very hot	240 - 250	500 - 525	7

Sub-editor *Debbie Quick*
Designer *Caryl Wiggins*
Project editor (food) *Karen Green*
Special feature photographer *Stuart Scott*
Special feature stylist *Wendy Berecry*
Special feature home economist *Alison Webb*

Test Kitchen Staff
Food director *Pamela Clark*
Associate food editor *Karen Hammial*
Assistant food editor *Amira Ibram*
Test kitchen manager *Elizabeth Hooper*
Senior home economist *Kimberley Coverdale*
Home economists *Emma Braz, Kelly Cruickshanks,
Sarah Hine, Sarah Hobbs, Naomi Scesny, Alison Webb*

ACP Books Staff
Editorial director *Susan Tomnay*
Creative director *Hieu Nguyen*
Senior writer and editor *Georgina Bitcon*
Senior editor *Liz Neate*
Chief sub-editor *Julie Collard*
Sub-editor *Debbie Quick*
Designers *Mary Keep, Caryl Wiggins, Alison Windmill*
Studio manager *Caryl Wiggins*
Editorial coordinator *Holly van Oyen*
Editorial assistant *Georgie McShane*
Publishing manager (sales) *Jennifer McDonald*
Publishing manager (rights & new projects) *Jane Hazell*

Production manager *Carol Currie*
Business manager *Sally Lees*

Chief executive officer *John Alexander*
Group publisher *Jill Baker*
Publisher *Sue Wannan*

Produced by *ACP books*, Sydney.
Colour separations by ACP Colour Graphics Pty Ltd,
Sydney. Printing by Dai Nippon in Hong Kong.
Published by ACP Publishing Pty Limited,
54 Park St, Sydney; GPO Box 4088, Sydney, NSW 1028.
Ph: (02) 9282 8618 Fax: (02) 9267 9438.
acpbooks@acp.com.au
www.acpbooks.com.au

AUSTRALIA: Distributed by Network Services,
GPO Box 4088, Sydney, NSW 1028.
Ph: (02) 9282 8777 Fax: (02) 9264 3278.
UNITED KINGDOM: Distributed by Australian
Consolidated Press (UK), Moulton Park Business Centre,
Red House Rd, Moulton Park, Northampton, NN3 6AQ
Ph: (01604) 497 531 Fax: (01604) 497 533
acpukltd@aol.com
CANADA: Distributed by Whitecap Books Ltd, 351 Lynn Ave,
North Vancouver, BC, V7J 2C4, Ph: (604) 980 9852.
NEW ZEALAND: Distributed by Netlink Distribution
Company, Level 4, 23 Hargreaves St, College Hill,
Auckland 1, Ph: (9) 302 7616.
SOUTH AFRICA: Distributed by PSD Promotions (Pty) Ltd,
PO Box 1175, Isando 1600, SA, Ph: (011) 392 6065

Great Italian Food
Includes index.
ISBN 1 86396 242 5
1. Cookery, Italian. I. Title: Australian Women's Weekly.
(Series: Australian Women's Weekly).
641.5945

© ACP Publishing Pty Limited 2002
ABN 18 053 273 546

Photographers: *Alan Benson, Kevin Brown, Scott Cameron,
Robert Clark, Joe Filshie, Rowan Fotheringham, Andre Martin,
Mark O'Meara, Rob Shaw, Brett Stevens, Robert Taylor, Jon Waddy.*

Stylists: *Lucy Andrews, Clare Bradford, Marie-Helene Clauzon,
Jane Collins, Rosemary de Santis, Georgina Dolling,
Carolyn Fienberg, Kay Francis, Jane Hann, Trish Heagerty,
Jacqui Hing, Katy Holder, Cherise Koch, Vicki Liley, Janet Mitchell,
Michelle Noerianto, Sarah O'Brien, Anna Phillips, Sophia Young.*

Cover: Spaghetti with pesto, page 66
Photographer: Stuart Scott
Stylist: Wendy Berecry

Back cover: Spinach, anchovy and olive pizza, page 96
Photographer: Stuart Scott
Stylist: Wendy Berecry